Too often, talk of baptis. ....
mechanics—which way is the right way—or policy—who is
in and who is out. With a poet's love of language and a large-
heartedness born of decades of pastoral ministry and deep
personal reflection, Steve Shoemaker instead calls us down
to the waters themselves, and shows us our reflection within
them. Steve reminds us the wealth of baptismal imagery
available to us through Scripture and tradition, revealing
many paths that lead us to the same, mysterious waters.

—*Scott Dickison*
Pastor of First Baptist Church of Christ
Macon, Georgia

With the wisdom and accessibility of a seasoned pastor and
preacher, Shoemaker offers us a beautifully written explora-
tion of both the mystery and the practicality of Christian
baptism. Anyone preparing for parish ministry should own
this book; it will prove a theological and homiletical resource
across Christian traditions. And for those of us yearning for a
deeper understanding of what it means to follow, to give our
whole selves to the "life-long apprenticeship" that is Christian faith, this book will be a valuable guide along the way.

—*Rev. Dr. Amy Butler, former senior minister*
Riverside Church in the City of New York
Founder, Invested Faith

Steve Shoemaker has the wisdom to know that in times such
as these, the human family needs to be grounded in memory,
identity, and the grace of God—and so he wrote a book
about Holy Baptism. Using his characteristically accessible
style to open the deepest truths, Steve gently pours into these
pages personal and biblical story, theology, and lines from

every literary genre, inviting us to wade into a deeper understanding of just how much and in how many ways "God loves us with water." This book, like its author, is a gift to the church in all its manifestations.

—*Rev. Ginger E. Gaines-Cirelli*
Senior pastor, Foundry United Methodist Church
Washington, DC
Author of Sacred Resistance: A Practical Guide to Christian Witness and Dissent

To Joy & Catherine
With such joy in our
friendship and gratitude
for years
together.

H. STEPHEN SHOEMAKER

[signature]

BAPTISM

A LIVING
SACRAMENT
of the
CHRISTIAN
LIFE

#10 Gleneagles Rd W
Statesville, NC 28625

Still
704-591-0192
Shoe1948@yahoo. come

Smyth & Helwys Publishing, Inc.
6316 Peake Road
Macon, Georgia 31210-3960
1-800-747-3016
©2022 by H. Stephen Shoemaker
All rights reserved.

Library of Congress Cataloging-in-Publication Data

Names: Shoemaker, H. Stephen, 1948- author.
Title: Baptism : a living sacrament of the Christian life / by H. Stephen
Shoemaker.
Description: First. | Macon, GA : Smyth & Helwys Publishing, 2022. |
Includes bibliographical references.
Identifiers: LCCN 2022011008 | ISBN 9781641733694 (paperback)
Subjects: LCSH: Baptism.
Classification: LCC BV811.3 .S56 2022 | DDC 234/.161--dc23/eng/20220404
LC record available at https://lccn.loc.gov/2022011008

To Stephanie Erin Leonard
and all whom I have had the holy honor of
baptizing through the years of my ministry

Also by H. Stephen Shoemaker

Seekers, Saints, and Sinners:
Life-changing Encounters with Jesus

Jesus Stories: Traveling toward Testimony

Being Christian in an Almost Chosen Nation:
Thinking about Faith and Politics

Finding Jesus in His Prayers

Strength in Weakness

Retelling the Biblical Story

Jekyll & Hyde Syndrome: A New Encounter with the Seven
Deadly Sins and Seven Lively Virtues

Godstories: New Narratives from Sacred Texts

Acknowledgments

I give thanks for the congregations I have served as pastor and who have blessed me with the holy honor of baptizing their people: Richland Baptist Church, Falmouth, Kentucky; Beverly Hills Baptist Church, Asheville, North Carolina; Crescent Hill Baptist Church, Louisville, Kentucky; Broadway Baptist Church, Fort Worth, Texas; Myers Park Baptist Church, Charlotte, North Carolina; and Grace Baptist Church, Statesville, North Carolina. They have been on the journey with me into the meaning of baptism.

As I wrote this book, I felt that it was a distillation of my theology passed through the prism of baptism. So I thank my many teachers through the years. I mention here Rollin Armour, Robert Handy, Lou Martyn, Raymond Brown, Henlee Barnette, Glenn Hinson, and, most gratefully, George Buttrick. And I thank the constellation of those who have taught me through their writings: Frederick Buechner, Reinhold Niebuhr, Karl Barth, Harry Emerson Fosdick, and more than I could ever name even with unlimited space.

I thank Sue, my wife and companion. As the word "companion" suggests, we have broken a lot of bread together in the writing of this book. She has not only been my word processor but has also been my thought processor as we talked about every page, almost every word, of this book.

I dedicate this book to Stephanie Erin Leonard and all whom I have had the holy honor of baptizing through the years. One Sunday at age sixteen, Stephanie announced to her parents, Bill and Candyce, "I think it's time for me to be baptized." And so she was, on Christmas Eve 1991. Her name and life represent the names and lives of all whom I have baptized. Not incidentally, her father, Bill J. Leonard, an American religion and Baptist history scholar, has taught me much about Baptist ways and practices.

And I thank you, Lord, in whose waters I have baptized and been baptized.

Contents

Preface

Baptists began their life in Europe in the sixteenth century. They were branded heretics and were persecuted, reviled, and killed for their belief that a person should be old enough to follow Jesus and call him Lord before being baptized. They were given the name "Anabaptists," meaning "Re-baptizers," a name not always uttered with kindness. As part of what is called the "Radical Reformation," they were also pacifists and opposed to the union of church and state.

It seems odd then that, among Baptists today, there is a dearth of new books on baptism and of new baptism hymns. Other denominations have provided far more. This book seeks to fill a little of this vacuum and encourage a lively discussion of the meaning and practice of baptism. It also seeks to enter the larger ecumenical discussion about baptism and join those at work on baptismal renewal in the church. As I develop ten key meanings of baptism, I hope this book will be of use to Christians and churches in all denominations, whatever their theology and practice of baptism.

I began by naming this book *Baptism: A Living Emblem of the Christian Life*. I considered the word "symbol" as well, but I chose the word "sacrament" for reasons I will develop in the book. Baptism is a living sacrament of the Christian life. May these reflections on baptism encourage us all in the living of our life in Christ.

God Loving Us with Water

In the most ancient of days, the places where water flowed—the fountain, the well, the oasis, the stream—were sacred places. Here was living water; here was the water of life. These were places of ceremony, and so are the waters of baptism.

Where did this book on baptism begin? At my own baptism? In the waters of my mother's womb? With the baptism of my mother and father, or with my baptizing grandfather? Or was it further back to the waters of the Jordan River where Jesus was baptized, with John doing the honors? In the waters of creation? As I have written this book, baptism has entered my dreams. It is so deeply embedded that it is in my unconscious life. Where do we begin? Let's start here.

It was the evening of our Easter Vigil at Broadway Baptist Church in center-city Fort Worth, Texas. The service began on the large front porch of the church. A fire blazed in a large cast-iron pot, the "Great Fire of Easter." After some spoken words, we lit our candles from the acolytes, who had taken their flame from the fire, and then we processed into the darkened sanctuary.

As the ancient introit was sung, we filled the sanctuary. We then heard a series of readings from Scripture telling of God's great acts of salvation and rescue, culminating in the reading of Jesus' baptism story from the Gospel of Mark. Several people were baptized, and then congregation renewed their baptismal vows: "Jesus Christ is Lord!" The Easter Gospel from John was read, the lights were raised, and alleluias rang out with the first hymn of Easter. Easter had begun, as it did with Mary, in the dark before the dawn.

After the service, I stood on the front porch of the church beside the fire. As people left the sanctuary, a stranger came up to me. He had gotten off the freight train nearby and seen the Great Fire of Easter. He made his way toward the church to investigate what was going on. He came into the service, sat on the back row, and watched the events with great interest, especially the baptism. There on the front porch he asked, "Would you baptize me?"

"Tonight?"

"Yes, tonight."

My mind went through a hundred calculations in an instant. "Of course," I said. "Sure, I will baptize you." I then grabbed a handful of people and asked if they would stay and become the congregation for this man who wanted to be baptized. They were more than glad to do so.

I led the man through the sanctuary to the baptismal changing area, handed him a clean, pressed white robe, then slipped my soggy robe back on. We entered the baptismal pool, and I baptized him. When he came up out of the water, I turned to the congregation sitting nearby in the choir loft and said, "If you affirm this man's baptism say,

'Thanks be to God.'" Their joyous voices rang through the mostly empty sanctuary.

As the man and I walked through the front door into the night air to say our goodbyes, I saw his beaming face. Off he went into the dark. I had been transported back into the book of Acts along the road to Ethiopia, where Philip met the Ethiopian eunuch who was on his way back home from Jerusalem. As the Ethiopian's chariot passed close to Philip, he saw that the eunuch was reading from Isaiah. The eunuch invited Philip to sit with him and teach him about the passage. As they talked, Philip told him how this text was fulfilled in a man named Jesus who opened God's temple to all. When they came to an oasis, the eunuch stopped and said to Philip, "Here is water. What hinders you from baptizing me?"

And Phillip, caught up in the Spirit, baptized him on the spot! He did not say, "Let me check with headquarters in Jerusalem." Then and there, they went down into the water and Philip baptized him. The text says that when they came up out of the water, the Spirit "snatched Philip away," on to his next place of witness, and "the man went on his way, rejoicing" (Acts 8:26-40).

This book is about baptism as a living sacrament of the Christian life and about how the manifold meanings of baptism depict the lived life of the Christian. It is about how we can, to use Walter Brueggemann's suggestive phrase, live with a "baptismal imagination." This phrase means more than a "baptized imagination"; it means an imagination fired with the images and meanings of baptism.

Early in Christian history, the cross became the central symbol of the Christian faith focused on the death and resurrection of Jesus. As central as the symbol of the cross is, I believe that baptism is the most comprehensive symbol of the Christian life as we seek to live out its transformational meanings. The first ten chapters of this book will explore ten of its meanings:

1. Baptism as Following Jesus
2. Baptism as Being the Beloved
3. Baptism as Naming Jesus "Lord"
4. Baptism as Turning and Entering the Kingdom of God
5. Baptism as Washing
6. Baptism as New Creation
7. Baptism as Anointing, Holy Spirit, and Calling
8. Baptism as Belonging to a Family of Faith, the Body of Christ
9. Baptism as Dying and Rising
10. Baptism as Resurrection and Eternal Life

In chapter 11, I offer "Pastoral Reflections on the Theology and Practice of Baptism." Following Baptist theologian Paul Fiddes, I place baptism within the context of the whole journey of the person into faith, which culminates in baptism,[1] a journey toward faith and within faith.[2] I will speak to the sacramental moments along this journey from childhood to adulthood and to the place of baptism in the worship life of the church.

The next chapter, chapter 12, is "Baptism as Sacrament: A Meeting Place with God." I discuss the spiritual appropriateness of calling baptism a "sacrament." Early Baptists did not shy away from the use of this word, and neither should we.

Chapter 13, the concluding chapter, is a collection of worship resources and liturgies for child dedication, confirmation and baptism, and baptismal renewal.

Now a word about the ecumenical spirit of this book. It is for all Christians who are seeking a deeper meaning for their lives. The transformational meanings of baptism reach across denominational, theological, and doctrinal lines. Chapter 11 seeks to enter the ecumenical conversation on the meaning of "one baptism," as the ecumenical movement has sought the unity Paul envisioned in Ephesians: "There is one body and one Spirit . . . one hope in your calling, one Lord, one faith, one baptism, one God and Father of us all who is above all and through all and in all" (Eph 4:4-6).

Tragically, baptism has been the occasion of battles over inclusion and exclusion and of persecution and death throughout the centuries. The goal of the ecumenical movement is to mend some of the rifts and promote the unity of the church Jesus that prayed might be one. The word "ecumenical" means "the whole world as the household of God." I write as a Baptist in one room of God's household to those in other rooms so that, together, we might be drawn into the vast Common Room of God's love.

In 1943, Karl Barth delivered a much-discussed lecture on baptism. In it he called for a renewal in the meaning and practice of baptism starting with the local congregation. The whole congregation, he said, must be involved in this endeavor through "pastoral care, instruction, preaching and open conversation."[3] I would be most happy if this book could aid in that conversation.

This book can be used for small-group and church-wide study, for the preparation of people considering baptism and desiring baptism. It may also be used as a guide for preaching on baptism, which was the wellspring of this book. It may be used for a Lenten season focusing on baptism and baptismal renewal, climaxing at Easter with baptism and the renewal of baptismal vows.

The latter chapters have pastors and church leaders especially in mind. I do not write as a professional theologian with expertise in these areas of sacramental theology and liturgy but as a working pastor who, for over forty-five years, has loved baptism and sought to give it a more meaningful and powerful place in the life of the congregation.

My introduction to the sacraments of the baptismal pool and Communion table came early. My earliest memory of church was as a child about four years old slipping surreptitiously back into my Southern Baptist church after Communion was served. I made my way to the Lord's Table and sipped from the thimble-sized glass Communion cups the unconsumed grape juice.

In the streets and countryside of England, John Wesley served the Eucharist to the unbaptized and unchurched because he believed that the Eucharist was a "converting sacrament." Who knows—perhaps God was beginning my conversion in that untransubstantiated Welch's juice.

I was baptized when I was about nine years old. It was Southern Baptist fashion in those days to encourage the baptism of elementary-aged children before they encountered the *real* sins and temptations of adolescence as they entered the "hormone zone." A woman wrote me a few years back. We had been baptized together in the same pool, the same night, at Ardmore Baptist Church in Winston-Salem, North Carolina. She said, tongue partly in cheek, "We didn't know what the heck we were doing that night!" She, however, has given much of her life to tending to Christ's "least of these," so even if we didn't know what we were doing, God did.

In my magnified memory of that night, I was filled with excitement. As I was lowered into the baptismal pool and lifted out again, blinking water from my eyes, I had the sense that some great adventure had begun—even when all I knew about theology and baptism could have scarcely filled one of those tiny glass Communion cups.

A few years back, the United Methodist Church of Christ designed their Lenten season as a Season of Baptismal Renewal with the theme "Remember Your Baptism and Be Thankful." In her recent book, liturgical theologian Gail Ramshaw develops the importance of the season of Lent becoming a season of baptismal renewal and preparation for baptism, where baptism becomes the key for forming our baptismal and Christian identity.[4] I hope this book will lead some of you to baptismal waters, and I hope it will lead others of you to remember your baptisms and be thankful.

John Calvin is often quoted as saying, "God knows we are creatures and so loves us in ways that we can understand: in bread and wine and water." This book is about how God love us with water.

Notes

1. Paul S. Fiddes, *Tracks and Traces: Baptist Identity in Church and Theology* (Eugene, OR: Wipf and Stock Publishers, 2003), 143, 183.

2. Ibid., 136.

3. Karl Barth, *Evangelische Theologie*, cited in George Beasley-Murray, *Baptism in the New Testament* (London: MacMillan & Co., 1962), 390.

4. Gail Ramshaw, *Word of God, Word of Life: Understanding the Three-Year Lectionary* (Minneapolis: Augsburg Fortress, 2019), 109–20.

Chapter 1

Baptism as Following Jesus

The first, most basic, and most concrete meaning of baptism is following Jesus. In the first chapter of Mark's fast-paced Gospel, before we can blink Jesus is calling Simon Peter and his brother Andrew at the seashore to follow him. "Follow me," he said, "and I'll make you fish for people." And "immediately" (one of Mark's favorite words), "they left their nets and followed him" (Mark 1:16-18). In the next two verses, Jesus calls James and his brother John, and they "followed him." The last words Jesus spoke to Peter as remembered in John's Gospel came at the seashore again; the Risen Jesus said to him, "Follow me." Follow me *on*.

In the book of Acts, the early description of being a Christian and following Jesus is called "the Way" (Acts 19:23). Baptism means placing your feet on the Way of Jesus and following.

I.

We can define Christian faith by a set of beliefs or doctrines, but at its core it is an action, a way of living as we follow the way of Jesus, as we follow *him*. The word often used for a follower of Jesus is "disciple." Literally it means "learner," but it is more than a learner of information; it is a learning of Jesus, a deeply personal kind of knowing. "Come to me," Jesus says, in that sublime passage in Matthew, "all you that are weary and carrying heavy burdens, and I will give you rest. Take my yoke upon you and learn from me; for I am gentle and humble in heart, and you will find rest for your souls" (Matt 11:28-9). It is not only a learning *from* him but a learning *of* him.

In *The Divine Conspiracy*, Dallas Willard prefers to use the word "apprentice" for disciples, describing an apprentice as "someone who has decided to be with another person, under appropriate conditions, in order to become capable of doing what that person does or to become what that person is."[1] I like this image of disciples as apprentices. It reminds us of who the master is; it implies that there will be trial and error, successes and failures in the learning; it reminds us that it will take time; and it suggests that what is learned is not just about doing but also about *being*—being like Christ.

What are "the appropriate conditions" for being a disciple? The first is dwelling in Jesus' words and letting his words dwell in us. It is about abiding in him as he abides in us. There is an alarming lack of such knowledge of Jesus in the American church today as it falls into heresies like nationalism and racism. Scholars in the new quest for the historical Jesus make a distinction between the religion *of* Jesus and the religion *about* Jesus. The religion *of* Jesus is about his teachings and doings, the Sermon on the Mount, his friendships with the outcasts and the poor, his moral teachings, and his ministry of healing and liberation. The religion *about* Jesus is about his coming from heaven as God's Son, his dying on the cross for our sins, and his defeat of death on Easter. We can focus so much on the religion about Jesus that we almost ignore the religion of Jesus.

The second appropriate condition is to learn of Jesus and how to follow him in the company of those who are trying to do the same. We learn better together; we need the company of those on the path with us and those who have sought to follow Jesus through the centuries.

Is there some laid-out plan for following him, some Google map of the Way? No, says Dietrich Bonhoeffer in his classic *The Cost of Discipleship*. "When Jesus calls," he writes, it is "Follow me, run along behind me! That is all!"[2]

What is the first step of turning to Jesus, the first step of following? Episcopal priest Samuel M. Shoemaker describes it this way: *"We surrender as much of ourselves as we can to as much of Christ as we understand."*[3] Then starts the marvelous adventure. We become capable of giving more and more of ourselves to Christ, and we learn more and more of Christ to give ourselves to.

It is a lifelong apprenticeship. The following will lead us to places we could never have imagined at the beginning. We will be changed along the way. We may find ourselves in strange company. There will be ups and downs. We will be confounded. There will be valorous moments of obedience and shameful betrayals, but Christ is by our side the whole way and will not abandon us. And, beyond our best hope some days, as we follow him we will become more like him, even though some days we cannot see it.

II.

A minister was preparing his sermon for the next day in the parsonage beside the church. The sermon text was 1 Peter 2:21: "For to this you have been called, because

Christ also suffered for you, leaving you an example, so that you shall follow in his steps." The minister's name was Henry Maxwell, and as he worked on the sermon there was a knock at the door. Standing there was a shabbily dressed man looking for work. As kindly as he knew how, Maxwell told him that he was terribly sorry but had no work to offer him. The man went on his way, and the minister returned to his sermon.

The next day at First Church, he masterfully delivered his sermon. The congregation nodded approval and appreciation. Then, suddenly and unexpectedly, the same shabbily dressed man made his way down the center aisle to the front of the church and began to speak.

He told the stunned congregation that he had been out of the work for ten months, walking from city to city looking for work. He said that he'd been in their city for three days with no luck in finding employment and that he had received no kindness or sympathy from anyone other than their pastor the day before. He was confused, he said to the congregation, about the lack of concern of good Christian people toward people like him. "What I feel puzzled about," he said, "is what is meant by following Jesus. What do you mean when you sing, 'I'll go with him, with him, all the way'?" He said a few more words, then collapsed on the sanctuary floor. He was carried to the parsonage where he could rest for a few days and recover his strength. Then, to everyone's shock, he died.

The next Sunday, Maxwell got up to preach, deeply shaken by all that had happened over the past week: the stranger's entrance into his life and the life of the church and his unexpected death. The man's question, "What do you mean by following Jesus?" had placed a question mark over everything in the minister's life and ministry.

That morning he confessed that he was shaken and then offered a challenge to the congregation: that they do nothing without first asking the question, "What would Jesus do?" After that, they should follow Jesus no matter the result. The minister said, "I will include myself in this company of volunteers and shall take for granted that my church will not be surprised at my future conduct as based on this standard of judgment."[4] A core group of the church from many walks of life agreed to the challenge. There were two requirements: (1) a time commitment of one year and (2) weekly small-group meetings for nurture, support, accountability, and guidance.

This story may be familiar to you. It's from Charles Sheldon's 1896 novel and spiritual classic, *In His Steps*. Some consider it an early social gospel novel because it sought to apply the teachings of Jesus to the social conditions of Sheldon's time. You may have read it long ago. It has been revitalized in more recent years in the merchandising of WWJD (What Would Jesus Do?) bracelets.

I read the book early in my life and put it aside. It seemed a bit simplistic and sentimental to me at the time, in my inflated sense of self. Then, in midlife and midcareer, I read it again, and it was as if it were a new book. The simplicity of the book now drove itself home to my heart. It felt like good news to my middle-aged soul.

There are times in our lives when we are given simplicity on the yonder side of complexity, what Paul Ricoeur calls "a second naivete." In his spiritual classic, *A Testament of Devotion*, Thomas R. Kelley wrote, "The last fruit [note "last"] of holy obedience is the simplicity of the trusting child, the simplicity of the children of God. It is the simplicity which lies beyond complexity. It is the naivete which is the yonder side of sophistication."[5]

The question "What would Jesus do?" is not as easy to answer as it sounds. We must "translate" Jesus from his time into ours. And we must know his words and what Jesus did! This question requires a leap of faith; we might get the answer right or wrong. But I do not think we can go far with Jesus in the Christian life without asking that question. It may bring trouble before it brings peace. It will put our bodies in new places. And it will require probing inner spiritual work and a community within which to consider the question.

Jürgen Moltmann, one of the most noted of twentieth-century theologians, became a follower of Jesus as a German prisoner of war in a Scottish POW camp. The Scottish chaplain had given him a Bible, and he began to read. His reading of the Bible, especially the Psalms and Mark's Gospel, opened him to Christ. In his autobiography, *A Broad Place*, he writes of following Jesus:

> I have never decided for Christ once and for all, as is often demanded of us. I have decided again and again in specific terms for the discipleship of Christ when situations were serious and it was necessary. But right down to the present day, after almost 60 years, I am certain that then in 1941, and there, in the Scottish prisoner of war camp, in the dark pit of my soul, Jesus sought me and found me.[6]

At one moment, the first following begins, and then day after day we choose the ways of Christ over and over again.

It was an early morning in Fort Worth when, in that drowsy first waking consciousness, I heard a voice saying, "Go join Michael." Michael Bell was a Black clergy friend. He had begun an ongoing early morning protest at an elementary school in a wealthy part of town to address the inequalities in the school system between white children and children of color. Other Black clergy and Black leaders joined him. The parents of the all-white school were not happy to be met by this group of protesters every morning as they took their children to school. That morning, out of the blue, came the words, "Go join Michael." I pulled on my suit and tie and went down the street to join them.

By the afternoon, I got a call from the assistant superintendent of schools, who said, "We got your license number. Why were you there?" The assistant superintendent was a friend who cared for the plight of the underserved children in the district, but he was, I think, a bit concerned for me. Members of my church who were parents of school-children in that school were not pleased. Was the voice I heard the voice of Christ, or conscience, or, as Scrooge said to the Ghost of Jacob Marley, merely "a bit of undigested potato"? That sort of prompting had never happened to me before. I wonder how many times I had not been sensitive to such promptings, much less followed them. But that day I decided, to use Moltmann's words, for the discipleship of Christ.

Sojourner Truth was an emancipated slave who worked for the abolition of slavery and the emancipation of women. When she preached, she was heckled. A woman preacher? An ex-slave preacher? Christ came to her in a vision to call her to follow. This is how she recalls the moment: She said to Christ, "I know and don't know you," which describes any authentic meeting with Jesus. Then she said, "You seem perfectly familiar; I feel that you not only love me, but that you have always loved me."[7] There too is a mark of an encounter with Jesus.

The meaning of baptism begins here, in the following of Jesus. There is a hymn that has become a favorite in some of my churches: "Will You Come and Follow Me?" It is from the Iona Community off the west coast of Scotland, written by John Bell and Graham Maule, and sung to the tune KELVINGROVE:

> Will you come and follow me if I but call your name?
> Will you go where you don't know and never be the same?
> Will you let my love be shown,
> Will you let my name be known,
> Will you let my life be grown in you and you in me? [8]

The Christian life is a sacrament of following and becoming like Christ in the world. It begins here.

Notes

1. Dallas Willard, *The Divine Conspiracy* (New York: Harper San Francisco, 1998), 282.

2. Dietrich Bonhoeffer, *The Cost of Discipleship* (New York: McMillan Co., 1963), 49.

3. Samuel M. Shoemaker, *How to Become a Christian* (New York: Harper, 1953), 71.

4. See Charles Sheldon's *In His Steps*, first published 1896 by Chicago Advance. More than 50 million copies have been sold.

5. Thomas R. Kelley, *A Testament of Devotion*, Doubleday Devotional Classics, vol. 14, ed. E. Glenn Hinson (Garden City: Doubleday & Company, Inc., 1978), 191.

6. Jürgen Moltmann, *A Broad Place: An Autobiography*, trans. M. Kohl (Minneapolis: Fortress, 2008), 30.

7. Olive Gilbert, *Narrative of Sojourner Truth* (New York: Arno Press, 1968), 67–69.

8. John Bell, "Will You Come and Follow Me?" *Common Ground: A Song Book for All the Churches* (Edinburgh: Saint Andrew Press, 1998), #148.

Chapter 2

Baptism as Being the Beloved

The Scriptures report that when Jesus was baptized, the sky was torn open, the Spirit descended like a dove, and a Voice from heaven said, "You are my Son, the Beloved, in whom I am well pleased," or, as I like to translate it, "in whom I take delight" (Mark 1:9-11).

I do not think there can be a more important image to hold in our hearts than this: God saying to us at our birth and at our baptism: "You are my beloved daughter; you are my beloved son. In you I take delight."

Baptism reconnects us with our belovedness. As Christians think about their identity as human beings, some begin in Genesis 3 with the story of Adam and Eve in Eden's garden, with the "fall" and "original sin." But we should begin where the Bible does, in Genesis 1, with God creating us in God's own image, blessing us and calling us "good"—that is, with "original blessing" not "original sin."

At Jesus' baptism, God spoke Jesus' belovedness to him. When I baptize, I recount the baptism in Mark and say to the one being baptized, "You are God's daughter/ son, the Beloved. In you God is well pleased, in you God takes delight." I hope we can hear those words at the depths of our being. We all have an unbroken center at the heart of who we are. It is our belovedness in the eyes and heart of God.

Henri Nouwen's spiritual classic, *Life of the Beloved*, has been a powerful message to us about our being "the Beloved." He wrote it first for a friend whom he met when the young man came to interview him. The young man was a skeptic and was surprised that Nouwen let him know that there was a place for skeptics in the spiritual realm of life. Later, the young friend came to him and said, "Why don't you write a book for me and my friends?" Thus came the book. Early on were these words:

> . . . all I want to say to you is "You are the Beloved," and all I hope is that you can hear these words as spoken to you with all the tenderness and force that love can hold. My only desire is to make these words reverberate in every corner of your being—"You are the Beloved."[1]

His book made these words reverberate in me and in thousands of readers. Those words of Christ's belovedness and ours are at the heart of my theology and spirituality.

So let's go back to the Jordan River when Jesus heard these words of his belovedness. Jesus, I believe, experienced his belovedness in God's eyes from his mother's arms. At the heart of his spirituality was what we could call his "Abba-experience," his experience of himself as the Beloved of God, whom he called *Abba*, the Hebrew child's first word for Daddy or Poppa. *Abba* was the Aramaic word Jesus used for his heavenly Father. It speaks of a relationship of intimacy, confidence, and trust. Everything he did and said came from this Abba-experience, from his earlier

words in the Sermon on the Mount to his last words on the
cross: "Abba, into Thy hands I commend my spirit" (Luke
23:46). He experienced his belovedness in his mother's
embrace, in his earthly father Joseph's love, in the beauty
of the Galilean flower-strewn hills, and in the temple in
Jerusalem when his parents took him on feast days. They
mediated to Jesus his belovedness.

When his parents lost him at age twelve on their trip to
Jerusalem and finally found him, on the third day of looking,
back in the temple talking with the amazed scholars, Jesus
said to his parents, "Did you not know I would be here
in my Father's house?" Or, as in some translations, ". . .
about my Father's business?" The Abba-experience was
there throughout his boyhood. In a hymn I wrote of the
historical Jesus of Nazareth, here is the first verse:

Praise the one who came among us,
God's own child from Galilee.
Home he was in field and temple,
Romping in his *Abba's* glee.
Alleluia, Alleluia! Praise the boy from Galilee.[2]

If however Jesus grew up with the deep sense of being
God's Beloved, it was spoken directly and powerfully to
him at his baptism. God called him Beloved, and the Spirit
anointed him for his mission as God's Son in the world.

At our baptism and as we remember our baptisms, we
should hear in the deepest places of our being God's words,
"You are my son/my daughter, the Beloved in whom I am
well pleased, in whom I take delight." I like the rephrasing
"take delight" because it conveys God's sheer joy in us,
not because we have done something right but because

we are simply the Beloved. We do not have to earn our belovedness.

Gordon Cosby once said that the chief duty of parents is "to enjoy their children." This taking joy in our children conveys in ways deeper than words, before any words, the grace of God.

Fred Rogers, the Presbyterian minister who became "Mr. Rogers" to millions of children, wrote this song for them—and us:

> It's you I like,
> …
> The way you are right now
> The way down deep inside you—
> Not the things that hide you . . .
> …
> It's you I like.[3]

We've heard all our lives that God loves us, but can we believe that God *likes* us? God takes sheer delight in us. I hope baptism helps you feel that delight.

Nouwen says that our spiritual quest in life, then, is to become the Beloved we already are. It does not happen all at once; we *become*. Becoming the Beloved is that longest of journeys, the sixteen inches from our head to our heart. As we shall see later in this book, part of the becoming is in discovering our call to be partners with God in God's purposes for the world, but it is deeper and earlier than that.

In the movie *Chariots of Fire*, Eric Liddell, a young Scottish man, has given his life to become a missionary in China, but he interrupts his preparations to be a missionary in order to train for the Olympics as a sprinter. His sister is not pleased at his delay in his missionary training and tells him so. Eric says to her, "I believe God made me for a purpose, but he also made me fast! And when I run I feel his pleasure."[4]

God wants us to feel the divine pleasure not only when we are fulfilling our calling but always, because we are the Beloved—as we feel the sun on our faces, run with joy, watch a sunrise, feel a cool summer breeze, make music, and do things we are created to do. When you are most deeply and fully you, you feel God's pleasure. God glories in our aliveness, our *us-ness*.

A priest from Belfast was visiting his uncle in Ireland. It was his uncle's eightieth birthday. One morning before dawn they went for a walk along Lake Killarny. As they stood side by side and watched the gorgeous sunrise, his eighty-year-old uncle suddenly turned and went skipping down the road, radiant, smiling ear to ear.

The nephew called to him, "Uncle Seamus, you look really happy."

"I am, lad," his uncle replied.

"Want to tell me why?" his nephew asked.

His uncle replied, "You see, me *Abba* is very fond of me!"[5]

And so is your Abba fond of you.

In Martin Luther's great Reformation hymn "A Mighty Fortress Is Our God," one verse is about our spiritual battle with the powers of evil in the world:

The Prince of Darkness grim,
We tremble not for him;
His rage we can endure,
For lo, his doom is sure;
One little word shall fell him.[6]

Satan, the "prince of darkness grim," is sometimes called "the Accuser." We hear accusing voices in our heads all the time: "You are no good. You'll never amount to anything. Why aren't you like _____?" These voices can crush our spirits. But there is that "one little word" that can fell the Accuser. Some Luther scholars say that for Luther that one little word was "*Baptizo*." *I am baptized!* Luther awoke every morning with the word "*Baptizo*"—I am baptized! So much is contained in the meaning of baptism, but at the most elemental level it means "I am the Beloved." What if we rose every morning with the words "I am baptized" on our lips and heard God say, "You are my Beloved in whom I am well pleased."

In the *Westminster Short Catechism*, perhaps the most well-known question is "What is the chief end of man?" And the answer: "The chief end of man is to glorify God and enjoy him forever." The enjoyment goes both ways.

Notes

1. Henri Nouwen, *Life of the Beloved* (New York: Crossroad, 1993), 26.

2. H. Stephen Shoemaker, *Jesus Stories* (Valley Forge, PA: Judson, 2016), 201.

3. Fred Rogers, "It's You I Like," *Neighborhood Archive*. neighborhood archive.com/music/songs/its_you_i_like.html

4. *Chariots of Fire*, film, dir. Hugh Hudson, written by Colin Welland, 1981.

5. Brennan Manning, *Abba's Child: The Cry of the Heart for Intimate Belonging* (Colorado Springs: NavPress, 1994), 65.

6. "A Mighty Fortress Is Our God," *Hymns for the Living Church* (Carol Stream, IL: Hope Publishing Co., 1990), hymn 11.

Chapter 3

Baptism as Naming Jesus "Lord"

When I baptize people, I invite them to share their faith by saying, "Jesus Christ is Lord," the historic baptismal vow.

Among the earliest confessions of faith in the New Testament was "Jesus is Lord." As Paul wrote in Romans, "If you confess with your lips that Jesus is Lord and believe in your heart that God raised him from the dead, you will be saved" (10:11). It is no magic formula; it is an alignment of one's life. Jesus said, "Not everyone who calls me 'Lord, Lord' will enter the kingdom of heaven, but only the one who does the will of Father in heaven" (Matt 7:21). To call Jesus "Lord" is to align your life with Christ and with the God who sent him.

A confession of faith combines the mind and heart. William Sloane Coffin writes, "Credo—I believe—best translates, 'I have given my heart to.'"[1] The mind and heart join in what Paul called "the obedience of faith" (Rom 1:5). There is the mind and heart of faith and, as we will see, obedient action too.

At baptism we name Jesus "Lord" and "Christ." What does it mean to call Jesus "Lord"?

I.

When you see LORD, capitalized, in the Old Testament, it is the translation of the holy name of God that God gave to Moses out of the burning bush: *Yahweh*, which is actually four consonants, YHWH (Exod 3:14). The vowels were added later. We guess at its pronunciation and translation. It is a form of the verb "to be," meaning something like "I Am Who I Am." Out of reverence for the holy name of God, Jewish people have substituted the name *Adonai*. It is a placeholder for the name of the Holy One, Yahweh.

Look at what we've done with this name of God through the centuries. It was first a Hebrew verb, then it became a noun, "Adonai," and then a presumably male noun, "Lord," thus taking on the character of a male authority figure. Some struggle, then, with the name "Lord" for its association with patriarchy.

Gail Ramshaw, a leading liturgical theologian, has worked extensively on the language of worship. For worship, she recommends translating "Yahweh" and "Lord" as "The Living One" when referring to God and Christ.[2] The phrase "Living One" is closer to the verb-like quality of Yahweh; it avoids the male centrism in our language; and it keeps God large in our minds, not small. Our language about God should strive to convey the largeness of the Mystery that is God. The meaning of Jesus as Lord changed after the resurrection. Before the resurrection, he was *rabbi, teacher, master* (the pre-resurrection translation of "Lord"). Now he is named Lord as part of the Divine Life of God. So Thomas, upon meeting the Risen Christ, exclaimed, "My Lord and my God" (John 20:28). Jesus the Living One was his divine Lord.

Jesus was also named "Christ," in the Hebrew "Messiah" or "Anointed One" of God. Jesus as the Anointed One of God was sent with a divine calling as God's Son in the world. Jesus as the Living One is master of our lives.

II.

What does it mean for us today to call Jesus "Lord"? It means more than we can name in the baptismal waters, more than what we conceive the first time we call him Lord. Toni Craven, professor of the Hebrew Bible at Brite Divinity School for many years, wrote of the elusive, virtually undefinable and untranslatable name of God given to Moses. Craven says that by giving Moses such a name God was saying, "Call me Yahweh. Follow me and I will teach you what this means." When we confess Jesus is "Lord," Jesus is saying, "Follow me and you will learn what this means."

Calling Jesus "Lord" means daily loyalty to him and daily obedience to his call to us to follow. The word "obedience" is tarnished today because we have seen such evil come from various forms of "obedience to authority." The obedience given to the authority of Jesus is, however, an obedience that leads to life. During the horror of the Third Reich and the capitulation of the German Church to Hitler, Dietrich Bonhoeffer wrote his classic, *The Cost of Discipleship*. In it he decried the prevalence of "cheap grace" in the church and said, "Only those who believe obey. . . . Only those who obey believe."[3]

I was leading a preparation for baptism class, and we were discussing what it means to call Jesus "Lord." One woman said, "To me it means Jesus is my Center." The

Teacher has become the "Rabbi within." And, as he is our Center, our center holds.

To call Jesus "Lord" means to take one path and not another, and this is the path that leads to life. To name Jesus "Lord" is to take the Sermon on the Mount seriously as our guide to life—even his most difficult command, "Love your enemies." Karl Barth defined "our enemy" as anyone who tempts us to return evil for evil, a temptation we face every day from the kitchen table to the water fountain to the boardroom.

Using Paul's metaphor for the Christian life, to call Jesus "Lord" means to take off some clothes like cruelty, falsehood, and hate and to put on new clothes like gentleness and kindness and forgiveness. It means to put *him* on! When asked about his religion, the Dalai Lama said, "My religion is simple. My religion is kindness." So was the religion of Jesus whom now we call "Lord."

III.

To call Jesus "Lord" is also a political act in the truest sense of the word *political*, that is, how we order our lives in the city, the *polis*, the public realm. To call Jesus "Lord" is to dethrone every other lord of our lives.

During the rise of Hitler in the 1930s, German Christians as a whole gave themselves over to Hitler and fell under his thrall. They succumbed to the dark energies of racism and nationalism. Race and nation had become gods and the *führer* was Lord. A small group of pastors and churches left what had become the "Reich Church" to form what they called the Confessing Church. Above all, what they confessed was *Jesus is Lord*, which meant Hitler was *not*. They issued what is called the Barmen Declaration. At the beginning it states its central purpose as concerning "the sin of idolatry and the lordship of Christ."

One article (8:11) of the Confession states, "Jesus Christ, as he is attested for us in Holy Scripture, is the one Word of God which we have to hear and obey in life and in death."[4] In another article (8:18) we read, "We reject the false doctrine, as though the church were permitted to abandon the form of its message and order to its own pleasure or to changes in prevailing ideological and political convictions."[5] These faithful Christians put their lives on the line to confess "Jesus Christ is Lord" and to live out what this means. In that company was Dietrich Bonhoeffer, the brilliant young German theologian who was executed on Hitler's order because of his opposition to Hitler and the Third Reich. He would not bow his knee to Hitler.

In the early days of Christianity in the Roman Empire, the confession of Christ as Lord meant exactly the same. They refused to say, upon the order of the Roman Emperor, "Caesar is Lord." Only Jesus is Lord, they confessed, and the blood of martyrs flowed.

The church in America today is being tempted, as the church has been tempted since Constantine, to give itself over to the political powers-that-be. Christian nationalism has become a movement of Christian supremacy, and "patriot churches" are springing up. We may need a new Barmen Declaration for our day.

The gospel of Jesus has political ramifications, but the church must not become a political religion and give itself over to political ideologies of the right or left, to what Paul called "gods that are no gods." The Welch poet Waldo Williams, in a stunning series of images of Jesus, describes Jesus as the one who "escapes the conscription in every army."[6] In a world of "lords," Jesus had one Lord, and now for us Jesus alone is Lord.

When Jesus said, "No one can serve two masters," he was literally correct. No one can. There is only one. He gave the example: no one can serve God and money. But there are many more lords vying for our souls. To say that Jesus is "Lord" means no one and nothing else is. Not calling Jesus "Lord" means everyone and anything can be lord, and these "lords" do not give life but take it away. As Bob Dylan sings,

> You're gonna have to serve somebody, yes you are
> You're gonna have to serve somebody,
> Well, it may be the devil or it may be the Lord
> But you're gonna have to serve somebody.[7]

Why not let this somebody be the One who gives you life?

In the baptismal waters, when we say "Jesus Christ is Lord," we cannot know all it will mean or can mean, but it is a moment more momentous than we realize. The Living One promises to be with us all the way, and he will teach us what this means.

Notes

1. William Sloane Coffin, *Credo* (Louisville, KY: Westminster John Knox, 2004), xv.

2. Gail Ramshaw, *Reviving Sacred Speech: The Meaning of Liturgical Language* (Akron: OSL Publications, 2000), 64.

3. Dietrich Bonhoeffer, *The Cost of Discipleship* (New York: Macmillan, 1959), 59.

4. *The Theological Declaration of Barmen*, in *The Book of Confessions* (Louisville: The Office of the General Assembly of the Presbyterian Church, U.S.A., 2004), 249.

5. Ibid.

6. Waldo Williams, "Between Two Fields," in Rowan Williams, *The Poems of Rowan Williams* (Oxford: Perpetua Press, 2002), 92–93; and Rowan Williams, *Open to Judgement* (London: Darton, Longman & Todd, 1984), 131.

7. Bob Dylan, "Gotta Serve Somebody," *Slow Train Coming*, Columbia Records, 1979.

Chapter 4

Baptism as Turning and Entering the Kingdom of God

Mark's Gospel announces the beginning of the ministry of Jesus in his preaching of the kingdom of God, the central theme of his life: "Jesus came into Galilee preaching the gospel of God and saying, 'The time is fulfilled, and the kingdom of God is at hand; repent and believe in the gospel'" (Mark 1:14-15, RSV). The great news (*euangelion*) of God that Jesus preached was the kingdom of God coming near. It was coming near in justice, joy, healing, reconciliation, and peace. We could enter it, and it came entering into us. But this entering entails within it a turning.

The New Testament Greek word for "repent" was *metanoia*, a change or turning of the mind. Marcus Borg interprets it as "to go beyond the mind we have."[1] The great Old Testament Hebrew word behind it was *shuv*, to turn, or return to God. Every turning to God is in the deepest sense a return to the One who made us and has loved us from the first. The turning John and Jesus preached was an individual turning and the turning of the nation. Both people and nations can lose their way.

The word "repent" may cause you to shrink back. It may bring a sick feeling in the pit of your stomach, a scalding sense of shame. We may laugh at the word to defend ourselves against some of the ways it has been used. The church has often used it in a shame-based way. Toxic shame attacks us at the level of our personhood. As John Bradshaw has taught us, it turns "You've done something wrong" into "There's something wrong with you"; "You've made a mistake" into "You are a mistake."[2]

Have you been driving down a road and suddenly heard a police siren behind you and seen the flashing lights in your rearview mirror? That feeling is the feeling some get when they hear the word "repent"—whether they've done anything wrong or not. But in fact, the sound of repentance is the sounding of trumpets over the canyon at dawn. It is a New World Symphony. It says, "You can change your life. You can begin anew. A new world is drawing near."

Baptism means turning. If we get on the wrong train, the first thing to do is to get off the train at the next stop and get on the right one. On a trip to Iona, the holy island off the coast of Scotland, I was taking the train back to Glasgow from the sea town of Oban. The train had a stop halfway where we were supposed to move up to a car nearer the front. The front cars of the train would continue to Glasgow. I missed the memo and stayed in my seat, preoccupied with something, probably a book I was reading. As the train began its journey, I looked out the window and said, "This looks familiar." After a few minutes I said, "This looks *real* familiar!" I was on my way back to Oban.

It is easy in our lives to get on the wrong train. We may not recognize it for a while, but, when we do, we are wise to get off as soon as we can and get on the right train. This is repentance.

Sometimes the turning happens when we have hit bottom with our addictions, compulsions, and self-sabotaging behaviors. The recovery movement speaks of "the gift of desperation," when things get desperate enough that we reach out for help. We are given the grace of turning.

Sometimes we turn because of some life-changing, life-rearranging encounter with beauty or truth or love. We then recognize how pale or meaningless our life has become. For Dorothy Day, the Catholic social reformer and saint, the moment came at the miraculous birth of her daughter, Tamar. In a poem about seeing an ancient sculpture of Apollo, the poet Rilke ends with the line: "You must change your life."[3] The poet Mary Oliver asks us the question of turning: "Tell me, what is it you plan to do with your one wild and precious life?"[4]

What we turn to is God and the kingdom of God that is drawing near. Because the kingdom of God is the kingdom of *God*, it cannot be captured in definitions or put in boxes, so Jesus used parables to help us see what the kingdom of God is like. The kingdom of God is like a great feast where all are invited, like a tiny mustard seed growing into a great tree, like a profligate son being welcomed home, like a woman finding her lost coin, like a pearl merchant finding the pearl of great price, like the despised Samaritan who saved the life of an injured Jew, like a shepherd leaving the ninety-nine and going after one lost sheep. We might be that sheep, that guest, that man on the road, that merchant, that woman. The parables help us imagine what the kingdom is and imagine what it would be like to enter it.

The kingdom of God is a realm, a reign, God's realm where God reigns. In his *Cotton Patch Gospel,* a translation of the Gospels into the language and place of the American South, Clarence Jordan translates the "kingdom of God" as "God's new order of the Spirit" and "the God Movement."[5] Wendell Berry calls it "The Great Economy."[6] Jesus scholars John Dominic Crossan and Marcus Borg call it "God's passion for earth."[7] After all, Jesus taught us to pray for the kingdom to arrive on *earth* as it is in heaven. Frederick Buechner speaks of it this way:

> The Kingdom of God is the time, or a time beyond time, when it will no longer be humans in their lunacy who are in charge of the world but God in his mercy who will be in charge of the world. It's the time above all else for wild rejoicing—like getting out of jail, like being cured of cancer, like finally at long last, coming home. And it is at hand, Jesus says.[8]

It is near, not far, as near as your own breath. Jesus said the kingdom of God is within you (Luke 17:21). It is something we enter and something that enters us. The *Gospel of Thomas* records Jesus saying that the kingdom is "inside us and outside us," that it is "spread out upon the earth, and people do not see it."[9] Christ has come to open our eyes, the eyes of the heart, not just our optic eyes but what e. e. cummings called "The eyes of our eyes."[10]

Baptism is the sign of our turning and entering the kingdom of God, the meeting of grace and faith. Baptist theologian James McClendon calls baptism an enacted sign of salvation, a sign of a "new orientation to the coming rule of God."[11] We are turning, we are reorienting ourselves, and our lives are entering the reign of God. We are saying, "We want to live our lives here, and not in any other kingdom of the world, not even our own." Richard Rohr says that when we pray "Thy kingdom come," we are praying "My kingdom go!" This is turning and entering the kingdom. And this kingdom is as near as ever.[12]

Notes

1. Marcus Borg, *Speaking Christian* (New York: HarperOne, 2011), 15.

2. John Bradshaw, *Healing the Shame That Binds You* (Deerfield Beach, FL: Health Communications, 1988).

3. Rainer Maria Rilke, "Archaic Torso of Apollo," poets.org/poem/archaic-torso-apollo.

4. Mary Oliver, "The Summer Day," *New and Selected Poems* (Boston: Beacon Press, 1994), 94.

5. Clarence Jordan, *The Cotton Patch Gospel: Matthew and John* (Macon: Smyth & Helwys, 2004), 7, 29.

6. Wendell Berry, "Two Economies," *The Art of the Commonplace: Agrarian Essays of Wendell Berry* (Berkeley: Counterpoint Press, 2002), 81.

7. Borg and Crossan have used this phrase often. It is developed in Marcus Borg, *The Heart of Christianity: Rediscovering a Life of Faith* (New York: Harper SanFrancisco, 2003), 126–46.

8. Frederick Buechner, "The Kingdom of God," in *The Clown in the Belfry: Writings on Faith and Fiction* (San Francisco: Harper San Francisco, 1992), 165.

9. *The Gospel of Thomas*, Sayings 3 and 113.

10. e. e. cummings, "i thank you God for most this amazing," *100 Selected Poems* (New York: Grove Press, 1954), 115.

11. James William McClendon, *Doctrine*, vol. 2 of Systematic Theology (Nashville: Abingdon, 1994), 386.

12. Rohr lecture, 2012, Myers Park Baptist Church, Charlotte, North Carolina.

Chapter 5

Baptism as Washing

Perhaps the most ancient meaning of baptism, as old as the rivers and streams, is washing—that is, being washed in water for the cleansing of our souls, our lives. Baptism means the washing away of sin and guilt, shame and remorse. This is how God loves us with water.

I.

Paul Ricoeur speaks of the earliest, almost archetypal image of sin and its effects as *being stained*. "What can wash away my sin . . . ?" Looking at her murderous hands stained with blood guilt, Lady Macbeth cries,

> Out damned spot. Out I say . . .
> Here's the smell of blood still.
> All the perfumes of Arabia will not
> sweeten this little hand.[1]

In the Gospel of Matthew, Pilate washes his hands to cleanse them of complicity in the execution of Jesus (Matt 22:24). One poet depicts him as "Pilate the fly," scrubbing his hands like the motion of a fly. In the Hebrew tradition, washing with water could cleanse one of ritual uncleanness. King David cried out in Psalm 51:2, consumed by his sin and guilt, "Wash me throughly from my iniquity and cleanse me from my sin." I retain the King James version's *throughly* here, for the washing is through and through.

God, through the prophet Isaiah, sounds the call to repentance: "Wash yourself; make yourselves clean; remove the evil of your doings from before my eyes; cease to do evil, learn to do good; seek justice, correct oppression, defend the fatherless, plead for the widow." And then God offers the grace-filled invitation: "Come now, let us reason together, says the LORD: though your sins are like scarlet they shall be made white as snow; though they are red like crimson, they shall be like washed wool" (Isa 1:16-18, RSV, adapted).

When we sin, or are sinned against, we feel stained. I was in a group conversation one day that turned ugly and cruel. To my shame, I said nothing. When I got home, I felt like I needed a long hot shower. I felt stained—stained by the conversation and stained by my silence.

There's something about sins we commit that leaves a stain. But the feeling of staining can also happen when we have been sinned against. Victims of rape have told me and others that they feel stained with a shame that can last and last. We yearn to be washed and made clean again.

The word "sin" can bring discomfort. We want, like Adam and Eve, to run and hide. To be sure, some have been battered by the word "sin" in church, as preachers have loved to preach about it. At its heart, sin is what harms ourselves and others; it can separate and estrange us from God, from others, and from our true selves. From the Iona Community's worship book comes this prayer of confession:

Before God, with the people of God,
I confess to my brokenness:
to the ways I wound my life,
the lives of others,
and the life of the world.[2]

II.

The forgiveness of sins rests on two truths. The first is the recognition of our own sin and the second is the belief that something can be done about it. The second helps us do the first. Both the Apostle's Creed and the Nicene Creed include these words near the end: *I believe in the forgiveness of sins.* Karl Barth wrote that every day, we ought to begin with the words, "I believe in the forgiveness of sins."[3]

Mark's Gospel says that John the Baptizer appeared "proclaiming a baptism of repentance for the forgiveness of sins," or, as the King James Version phrases it, "the remission of sins" (Mark 1:4). In George MacDonald's nineteenth-century sermon, "The Remission of Sins," he says that the truest meaning of the phrase is the "sending away of sins" (the most Hebraic understanding of the words).[4] Baptism helps send individuals sins away.

Baptism also points to the sending away of sin itself. On the day after baptizing Jesus, John saw him approaching and said, "Here is the Lamb of God who takes away the sin [singular] of the world" (John 1:29). Here is sin not as a catalogue of individual sins but rather as a power that can overtake our lives. (This was Paul's concept of sin too.) Baptism—John's, Jesus', and ours—is a living sacrament of the power of Christ to defeat the power of sin itself. As Reinhold Niebuhr taught, grace is not only pardon; it is *power* too.[5] Baptism joins us with Christ's power in the overcoming of sin.

Some ask, and others argue endlessly, "How does the Lamb of God take away the sin of the world?" The sacred poetry of John's words points to the ineffable miracle: *What we cannot do for ourselves Christ has done for us.* We cannot wash away our own sin nor rid the world of its tired and terrible sins, but Jesus is the Lamb of God who takes away the sin of the world.

III.

Baptism is also the washing away of the residue of sin: guilt, shame, remorse, and regret. We can be crippled by these. Who has not been weighed down by some of them? Who has not said, "I wish I had been a different person then"?

God washes away these debilitating conditions of the soul. Scripture speaks not only of the washing away of sins but also of the "cleansing of the conscience" (Heb 9:9). An old hymn tells of Jesus who "gives the laboring conscience peace."[6] Such is the cleansing of the conscience. Psychologists speak of the "tyrannical conscience," one that keeps us in the thrall of misery. It can come early in our lives and be our lifelong oppressor. Sometimes our "conscience" is shaped more by the world around us than by the God who made us.

Another way of talking about this is the need to differentiate between "true guilt" and "false guilt." True guilt is the pain we feel when we have not lived up to our deepest and best values and thus wounded ourselves, others, and the life of the world. "False guilt" is the pain we are made to feel by our own culture, family, or religion. It is imposed on us from outside.

Madeleine L'Engle, author of *A Wrinkle in Time*, tells in her memoir *The Summer of the Great-Grandmother* of a period in her life when she was—all at the same time—trying to care for her aging mother, trying to be a perfect daughter and wife and mother and grandmother, and trying to fulfill her vocation as a writer. Impaled upon the false guilt of trying to be perfect in all these areas, she grew exhausted, irritable, and despondent. Then one day a friend came to her for counseling, and Madeleine heard herself saying words to her friend that she herself most needed to hear: "I don't think real guilt is ever much of a problem for us. It's false guilt that causes the trouble."[7]

Such is true for many of God's children. Baptism is the sign that God washes away not only true guilt but false guilt too. Call it the "sacrament of imperfection." It helps us live in the freedom of God's love and abiding grace.

Martin Luther arose in the morning with the words, "I am baptized." It also means "I am forgiven."

When I have taught classes in preparation for baptism and we have talked about baptism as "washing," I have said, "In the Baptist mode of baptism, you don't get a little wet; you get *all* wet! And God doesn't forgive some of you sins but all of them." We are washed "throughly." Baptism is the living sacrament of the forgiveness of sins, not just once but every day and forever.

One of the wonderful new baptism hymns is by hymnist Ruth Duck. It sings of baptism as washing: "Wash O God, our sons and daughters / Where your cleansing waters flow.... We your people stand before you, / water-washed and Spirit-born."[8]

Notes

1. William Shakespeare, *Macbeth*, Act V, sc. 1.38.

2. Iona Abbey Worship Book (Glasgow: Wild Goose Publications, 2001), 16.

3. Karl Barth, *Dogmatics in Outline* (New York, Philosophical Library, 1949), 150.

4. George MacDonald, "The Hope of the Gospel," Project Gutenberg, gutenberg.org/files/14453/14453-h/14453-h.htm.

5. Reinhold Niebuhr, *The Nature and Destiny of Man*, vol. 2 (New York: Charles Scribner's Sons, 1964), 107–24

6. Isaac Watts, "I'll Praise My Maker While I've Breath" (1719).

7. Madeleine L'Engle, *The Summer of the Great-Grandmother* (New York: Seabury Press, 1979), 50.

8. Ruth Duck, "Wash O God, Our Sons and Daughters," *The United Methodist Hymnal* (Nashville: United Methodist Publishing House, 1989), #605.

Chapter 6

Baptism as New Birth and New Creation

As a living sacrament of the Christian life, baptism means new birth and new creation. Birth speaks to personal transformation, and new creation speaks to the transformation of the world.

I.

Jesus' nighttime meeting with Nicodemus in John's Gospel focused on personal transformation, of being "born again," born *anothen*, born anew, born from above. Let's ponder the mystery of the new birth. Nicodemus had watched Jesus, seeing what he did and hearing what he said. Coming under the cover of the night, he said to Jesus, "Rabbi, we know that you are a teacher who has come from God; for no one can do these signs that you do apart from the presence of God" (John 3:2). Through God's prevenient grace, the grace that goes before, Nicodemus's eyes were opened to the work of God in Jesus.

He was unprepared, however, for Jesus' first words: "Truly, truly, I say to you, unless one is born again they cannot see the kingdom of God" (John 3:3). Nicodemus answered, in effect, "Isn't it a little too late for that? Can one enter a second time into his mother's womb?" Drawing him in more deeply, Jesus rephrased the matter: "Truly, truly, one cannot enter the kingdom of God without being born of water and the Spirit." Now we are being drawn into the heart of the matter. Everyone is born amid the waters of their mother's womb, but we need something more: to be born of the Spirit, to have a new birth, a second birth, this one from above. There is transformation here.

Jesus likened the mystery of the new birth to the mysterious movement of the wind. The words for the Spirit in the Bible, *ruach* in the Hebrew, *pneuma* in the Greek, mean spirit, wind, and breath, all three. Jesus says, "The wind blows where it will and you hear the sound of it, but you do not know where it comes from or where it goes" (John 3:8). That's the work of the Spirit in the new birth. Some try to narrow down this work to one kind of experience, but we cannot bottle the wind or lasso the Spirit. There is a wildness about the Spirit that we cannot domesticate— though we try.

For some the new birth blows in like a hurricane, rearranging everything. For others it comes like a sweet summer breeze fragrant with flowers. For some it comes in an instant, and for others it happens gradually, like the slow coming of the dawn or a flower turning its face almost imperceptibly toward the sun.

Some evangelists and preachers have said that if you cannot pinpoint the exact moment you were saved, you have not been saved. But this is a presumptuous confining of the Spirit to one way of working. Moreover, it creates salvation anxiety where there should be none. The mystery of the new birth is held in the mystery of God. Some know the moment of their conversion; others know only that God has been at work all along.

In the children's classic *The Velveteen Rabbit*, two toys in the boy's playroom, the wise old Skin Horse and the new Velveteen Rabbit, are talking about what it means to be REAL. The Rabbit asks, "Does it happen all at once, like being wound up . . . or bit by bit?" The Skin Horse says, "You become . . . !" It happens, he tells the Rabbit, "when you have been loved for a long time, REALLY loved."[1] That's how we become real: in the love of Christ who has loved us from the first and will love us forever.

For most of us, the new birth is a process of becoming. As one theologian put it, it takes a lifetime of conversions to become the new creation God has made us to be. It is being born again and again.

The Spirit works as the Spirit needs to work in our individual, unique lives. There are no cookie-cutter conversions. Every new birth is different. For Paul, his conversion on the road to Damascus, from "breathing threats and murder" against Christians to giving his life to Christ, was an immediate, life-changing experience. Saul the persecutor became Paul the apostle. His life was divided into two: B.D., before Damascus, and A.C., after Christ. Flannery O'Connor wrote of Paul's conversion, "I reckon the Lord knew the only way to make a Christian out of that one was to knock him off his horse."[2]

Dag Hammarskjöld, the secretary general of the United Nations in the 1960s, kept a spiritual journal now gathered in *Markings*. He writes of a different kind of conversion:

> I don't know Who—or what—put the question. I don't know when it was put. I don't even remember answering. But at some moment I did answer Yes to

someone—or something—and from that hour I was
certain that existence is meaningful and that therefore,
my life in self-surrender had a goal.[3]

The mystery of the new birth should never be narrowed
to a formula. God listens for our unique soulfulness and
comes into our lives just as we need.

II.

This transformation, however, is not only personal; it is also
the transformation of the world. Jesus called this transformation of everything "the kingdom of God." We enter the
kingdom, and the kingdom enters us. There is Christ in us,
but there is also an entering into Christ and Christ's realm
of transformation that is larger than we can ever imagine.

And what happens when we enter into Christ is *change*!
Jesus said, "Unless you *change* and become like children
you will never enter the kingdom of heaven" (Matt 18:3).
To become as a child means to live with wide-open need
and wide-open wonder. This is how we enter, in our need
and in our wonder. Such change is not only transforming
us but also transforming the world.

The second meaning of baptism in this chapter, then,
is what Paul called "the new creation." It was his way of
speaking of the kingdom of God as he sought to translate the meaning of the gospel to the Hellenistic mind. In
the new creation, transformation is personal, social, and
cosmic. In his hymn of the new creation in 2 Corinthians,
he writes, "Therefore, if anyone is in Christ, there is a new
creation. Everything old has passed away; see, everything
has become new!" (5:17). The translation many of us grew
up with was "If any man is in Christ, he is a *new creature*."
The emphasis was on personal transformation. But Paul's

vision was larger. The newer translations are truer: "Therefore, if anyone is in Christ, *there is a new creation!*"

The old creation is passing away, and the new creation is on the way. The old creation is marked by division, distrust, fear, and hatred. But these walls are coming down, and in their place reconciliation is happening. Distinctions like race, gender, and class are losing their power to divide. Near the end of Galatians, Paul pronounces the end of such division. In Galatia, the main issue was the division between Jew and Gentile. In "large letters" in his "own hand," Paul writes, "NEITHER CIRCUMCISION NOR UNCIRCUMCISION IS ANYTHING; BUT A NEW CREATION IS EVERYTHING!" (Gal 6:11, 15).

This is happening before our eyes if we can only see. A Berlin Wall comes down. Apartheid in South Africa is overcome. Civil rights legislation is passed in the US Congress. A racial reckoning after George Floyd's death is forcing us to face systemic racism and racial inequity, and white lives are being changed. In *Loving vs. Virginia*, the Supreme Court makes marriage between different races legal for the nation. Gay people are being freed from legalized discrimination, and those forbidden to marry in the old creation are being married in the new. The glass ceiling for women is being shattered as they take leadership positions never possible before.

Paul Tillich wrote these luminous words about the new creation and our participation in it:

> We want only to show you something we have seen and to tell you something we have heard: That in the midst of the old creation there is a New Creation, and that this New Creation is manifest in Jesus who is called the Christ . . . . We want to communicate to you an

experience we have had that here and there in the world and now and then in ourselves is a New Creation.[4]

For the Apostle Paul, the main theme of the new creation was *reconciliation* with God, with others, and with our own deepest selves. In the deepest spiritual sense, it is reunion. So Paul goes on in his new creation hymn: "All this is from God, who reconciled us to himself through Christ, and has given us the ministry of reconciliation" (2 Cor 5:18). Then he concludes with a call and a plea: "So we are ambassadors for Christ, since God is making his appeal through us; we entreat you on behalf of Christ, *be reconciled to God*" (5:20).

It is a reconciliation already accomplished in Christ. We need only receive it as a gift, the gift of all gifts, and live it out. When we are baptized, we receive this gift and become emissaries of the kingdom of God and ambassadors of the new creation.

There is a movie from 1999 called *The Straight Story*. It is based on a true story of a man named Alvin Straight who rode his riding lawn mower 240 miles across Iowa to Wisconsin to visit his ailing brother. They had become estranged and not spoken to each other in years. One day Alvin heard of his brother's grave illness and decided to do all he could do to restore the relationship. Alvin was up in years and no longer had a car or a driver's license, so he took off across Iowa on his riding lawn mower. He rode through scorching heat and shivering cold, in all kinds of weather and conditions.

Finally, he arrived at his brother's house, walked up to the front porch, and yelled his brother's name through the screen door. Inside the house, his brother gave a yelp of joy and called out, "Is that you?" That is the sound of reconciliation, the joyful cry of the new creation.

Christ has done something like that for us, Paul says, and when we hear the sound of his voice we come running. And now, Paul says, we get to join in the holy work of the new creation.

At baptism we give witness to the new birth and the new creation. There is something thrilling about the word "new." Something is happening that we did not think possible. God's new has come into our lives and the life of the world.

The new birth is about opening, and everything wants to open. We open ourselves to the life-bringing Spirit. The new creation is about reunion with God, self, others, and life itself. Now we can *live* with all our heart, mind, soul, and strength.

Notes

1. Margery Williams, *The Velveteen Rabbit* (Philadelphia: Running Press, 1981), 14.

2. Flannery O'Connor, *The Habit of Being* (New York: Vintage, 1979), 354–55.

3. Dag Hammarskjöld, *Markings* (New York: Knopf, 1966), 201.

4. Paul Tillich, *The New Being* (New York: Charles Scribner's Sons, 1955), 18.

Chapter 7

Baptism as Anointing, Holy Spirit, and Calling

All my life I have pondered the meaning of "vocation" and "calling." Such words hold for me an unfathomable fascination. Perhaps it is because I grew up in a family of ministers; my father was a minister of music, and my grandfather and uncle were both ministers.

In 1 Samuel in the Hebrew Scriptures, young Samuel is given by his parents to God and lives in the temple area, serving Eli the priest. One night God calls to him three times: "Samuel, Samuel." He at first thinks this is Eli calling him, but Eli says he hasn't and tells Samuel to lie back down. The third time Samuel hears God call his name, he says, "Speak, LORD, for your servant is listening." (See 1 Sam 3:1-10.)

I grew up in church; talk about the call of God was always in the air. Like Samuel, I may have heard a number of voices over the years, but there was a time when I said in my own way, "Speak, Lord, for your servant is listening."

Today I realize that I was looking at the meaning of calling through the wrong end of the telescope. I was seeing calling in the smaller sense of "church vocation." We called it "full-time Christian service," referring to people like ministers and missionaries. Now I look through the right end and see vocation in a much broader sense, as joining in partnership with God and God's purposes in the world. A poet, a physician, a farmer, a mother or father, a teacher, and many more have callings.

In an increasingly secular age, some might question the idea of a calling from God. Does God still call us to places of meaning and significance? Do we believe in such a God? It is important, then, that as we ponder the meanings of baptism, we address these three: anointing, Holy Spirit, and calling.

As I baptize today, I renew the ancient practice of the church to include the laying on of hands as part of the baptismal rite. The laying on of hands was an ancient sign of the anointing of the Holy Spirit in a person's life. As the person comes out of the water, I lay hands on them and offer a prayer of blessing and commissioning.

I.

The Spirit who anoints us calls us into partnership with God and with what God is up to in the world. So I begin here: *Baptism is the ordination of all believers to be ministers of the good news of God in Christ.* Traditionally the church has ordained and laid hands on those with specific callings to serve the church: ministers, deacons, elders. Historically, we were told that these were the ones with a "vocation." But God is calling the whole people of God to the vocation of ministry, and baptism with the laying on of hands is its sacred sign. The clergy have no corner on calling.

In a novella by Andre Dubus, a character named Joe is looking back over his life as a priest. Some young priests, he said, went to seminary to move up in the ranks like young officers. Others went, he said, to work out their neuroses. But most, he said, went because they wanted "to live their lives with God." He said these are the ones who had a "vocation."[1] That is the heart of our calling: to live our lives with God and then see where that love takes us.

Love is at the heart of vocation. Jesus' greatest commandment says to love God and love our neighbor. This is the calling of the church as well. H. Richard Niebuhr in *The Purpose of the Church and Its Ministry* says that the church's purpose is "the increase in the love of God and neighbor."[2]

II.

As Jesus was baptized, the Spirit descended on him in the form of a dove, anointing him for his mission as God's Son in the world. So we at our baptisms are anointed and called to be partners with God and God's mission in the world.

In ancient Israel, the king was anointed as "God's son" to preside over the nation; in the kingdom of Jesus, we are all anointed and called into the service of God's love in the world. From its beginning, the Eastern Orthodox Church has anointed the one being baptized. In the New Testament church, the laying on of hands was practiced to signify the anointing of the Holy Spirit. In Acts 6, the church needed to create a new set of ministers to serve the church. They called these ministers "deacons," and the whole church laid hands on them. The laying on of hands is one of the most important sacraments of the church, and at baptism we all can share in this sacred action. As we will see in chapter 11 below, in today's ecumenical discussion about baptism, the consensus is to return to the ancient practice of the laying on of hands at baptism.

Baptism as the ordination of all believers to be ministers of Christ was signaled in the Protestant Reformation's focus on "the priesthood of all believers." At baptism we are called, anointed, and ordained to be God's priests in the world, offering God's grace to others and becoming priests to one another.

At one time, a person's vocation was tied to their station in life: birth order, education, place in society, gender, and so on. So vocation was placed under the Doctrine of Creation. Today, theologian Miroslav Volf places the theology of vocation under the doctrine of the Holy Spirit.[3] The Holy Spirit can call anyone to any vocation, male or female, rich or poor. And the Spirit can call us to one vocation at one point in our lives and to another at another time in our lives.

In the Celtic Christian tradition, the symbol of the Holy Spirit is the Wild Goose. Not a gentle dove resting on your shoulder but a wild goose leading you out and leading you on to where God most needs you to go. We will not return unchanged!

Every Christian, then, has a vocation, a calling. In the Protestant Reformation, Luther offered a revolutionary new way to understand "vocation." At that time it was the priest, the monk, the nun who had a vocation. Luther said that we all have a vocation. The cobbler making shoes serves God as truly as a monk saying his prayers.

III.

Vocation is a "being sent" by God into the world. On Easter evening, the risen Christ appeared to his disciples huddled in fear behind locked doors. "Peace be with you" were his first words. Then he said it again—"Peace be with you"—for they, like us, need to hear those words over and over (John 20:21-22).

Now came the call: "As the Father sent me, so send I you." We too are being sent. In the Greek language the word for "sent" is the same as the word for "apostle". An apostle is one who is sent. So Jesus "apostled" his disciples, and he is "apostling" us today. The "apostolic church" is the church sent into the world as God sent Jesus.

Jesus' next action was this: he blew his own breath on his followers and said, "Receive the Holy Spirit." We, like them, need the anointing of the Spirit as Christ sends us into the world. Baptism with the laying on of hands is the sign of this anointing.

IV.

There is a dimension of calling that is at the level of person-hood, of *being*, of becoming the person God created and called us to be. As long ago as the second century CE, Greek bishop Irenaeus observed that the glory of God is "the human being fully alive." One's vocation then, has always entailed a discovering of one's true self. Jesus accompanies us on this journey. Such a journey is neither quick nor easy. The poet May Sarton wrote,

> Now I become myself. It's taken
> Time, many years and places,
> I have been dissolved and shaken,
> Worn other people's faces . . . .[4]

Parker Palmer, in his book *Let Your Life Speak: Listening for the Voice of Vocation*, writes of the mistakes he made earlier in his life when he thought his vocation came in imitating the lives of people he most admired. But our true vocation comes, he says, as we listen to our own life and discern what God is calling us to be and to do.[5] The early imitation of our heroes and saints may help pave the way for living out our own vocation, but imitation is not our vocation.

There is a Hassidic story about when Rabbi Zusya, now late in life, says, "In the coming world they will not ask me: Why were you not Moses? They will ask me, Why were you not Zusya?"[6] In another rabbinic story, Josef is crying out to God, "Make me like Abraham!" God replies, "I already have an Abraham. I want a Josef." Who is the "you" God is calling you to be?

In Gail Godwin's novel *Evensong*, a young Episcopal priest, Margaret Bonner, is tossing and turning about her vocation as a priest. A fellow priest writes her a letter and says, "Something is your vocation if it keeps making more of you."[7] That's what our true calling does; it keeps making more of us.

V.

Finally, vocation always involves a way of serving the world. When Jesus returned to his hometown of Nazareth to preach his inaugural sermon, he took up the scroll of Isaiah and read, "The Spirit of the Lord is upon me, because he has anointed me to bring good news to the poor. He has sent me to proclaim release to the captives and recovery of sight to the blind, to let the oppressed go free, to proclaim the year of the Lord's favor" (Luke 4:18-19). The anointing Spirit of God calls us to befriend the poor, set people free, open blind eyes.

Frederick Buechner's words about vocation have been most helpful to my understanding. God calls us, Buechner writes, to that meeting place between our great joy and the world's great need. "Neither the hair shirt nor the soft berth will do. The place God calls you is the place where your deep gladness and the world's deep hunger meet."[8]

We use words like *job, work, profession, career*. Our sacred calling may or may not have anything to do with those words. Your calling may have a paycheck attached, but it would be your calling with or without the money. It may be what poet Donald Hall calls your "life-work," where your work is also your devotion.[9] It may be an "avocation," a calling outside your work.

Parker Palmer writes in his own way about calling as the joining of joy and service to the world: "For me, the heart of the spiritual quest is to know 'the rapture of being alive,' and to allow that knowledge to transform us into celebrants, advocates, defenders of life wherever we find it."[10] Now *that* is true vocation. The joy of such a calling gives us holy energy to be the celebrants, advocates, and defenders of life the world needs.

As I baptize people and they rise from the water, I lay hands on them and say,

> Go now, as God's son/daughter,
> called to be a minister of the love of Christ. And as you go,
> May the Lord bless you and keep you,
> may the Lord make his face to shine upon you and be gracious to you,
> may the Lord lift up his countenance upon you
> and *through you* give the world peace.

Notes

1. Andre Dubus, "Adultery," *Selected Stories* (Boston: David R. Godine Publishers, 1988), 438.

2. H. Richard Niebuhr, *The Purpose of the Church and Its Ministry* (New York: Harper and Brothers, 1956), 27.

3. Miroslav Volf, *Work in the Spirit: Toward a Theology of Work* (New York: Oxford University Press, 1991).

4. May Sarton, "Now I Have Become Myself," *Selected Poems of May Sarton* (New York: W.W. Norton, 1978), 191.

5. Parker Palmer, *Let Your Life Speak: Listening for the Voice of Vocation* (San Francisco: Jossey-Bass, 2000).

6. Martin Buber, *Tales of Hasidim: The Early Masters* (New York: Schloken Press, 1975), 251.

7. Gail Godwin, *Evensong* (New York: Ballantine Books, 1999), 12.

8. Frederick Buechner, "Vocation," *Wishful Thinking: A Theological ABC* (New York: Harper & Row, 1973), 95.

9. Donald Hall, *Life Work* (Boston: Beacon Press, 1993), 8.

10. In Parker Palmer, *The Active Life: A Spirituality of Work, Creativity and Caring* (San Francisco: Jossey-Bass, 1999), 8.

Chapter 8

Baptism as Belonging

Baptism means belonging to a family of faith, the body of Christ. One of the greatest of human needs is the need to belong. When delivering lectures to aspiring children's book writers, Theodor Geisel, better known as Dr. Seuss, would say that a children's book should address at least one of what he called "the seven needs of children." Near the top of the list was "the need to belong."[1] Baptism is about belonging to God and belonging to a community of faith.

I.

A child has a physical, emotional, and spiritual need to belong. God placed Jesus into the hands of a family with a mother and father and within a Jewish community of faith. At home and synagogue, he found a place of belonging.

Perhaps the most poignant question of our lives is "Where do I belong?" There is a reason so many children's classics—and adult classics too—have as the main character an orphan looking for home and a place to belong. One might say there is an orphan in all of us, homesick for home, searching for our true identity.

Here is one of the meanings of redemption. In his beautiful little book, *Redemption*, theologian Alister McGrath discusses the major meanings of redemption in the Christian faith. The first is "Being Wanted."[2] Paul wrote of this dimension as receiving adoption as children of God: "But when the fullness of time had come, God sent his Son . . . so that we might receive adoption as children. And because you are children, God has sent the Spirit of his Son into our hearts, crying, 'Abba! Father!'" (Gal 4:4-5). Jesus is the head of God's Universal Adoption Agency!

Like children we all need to hear and experience the words "You are wanted." God places us in families so we might experience the joy of being wanted. Tragically, families do not always convey this redemptive environment. Sometimes parents use this most basic need in ways that manipulate or abuse their children. God created the church as a family of faith so that all might experience spiritual and emotional belonging. John Milton's definition of learning in his essay *Of Education* goes like this: "The end of learning is to repair the ruins of our first parents by regaining to know God aright and out of that knowledge to love Him, to imitate Him, to be like him."[3]

The church is where we learn to know God aright so that we might love God and live in that love.

II.

Jesus came not only to start a movement—the movement of the kingdom of God—but also to form a community. It began with the calling of the Twelve and then moved to a larger circle of disciples that included women too: Mary Magdalene, Joanna, and Susanna (Luke 8:1-3).

The child in a church is given a number of sacraments and sacred actions that communicate belongingness: infant baptism, child dedication, what early Baptists called "the devotion of children," first communion, and confirmation.

As Christ gathered children to him and blessed them, so do we.

Baptism is the living sacrament of belonging to God, to Christ, and to a family of faith, so the rite of baptism is best practiced in the presence of a family of faith, followed with Communion shared by all. At one church, I baptized the "discipleship class," who had been readied for baptism, in a lake after Sunday worship. As each baptized young person came to the shore, their family was there to embrace them and wrap them in a blanket. Then all the congregation did the same by encircling them and sharing Communion together.

III.

We might think of the church with the help of a Venn diagram. There are three interlocking circles. The top circle is "Belonging," the circle down to the left is "Believing," and the circle down to the right is "Behaving" or, to use Marcus Borg's word, "Beloving."[4]

Belonging comes first. It is at the top because we best learn the beliefs that undergird faith and life within a community of belonging. That is where we learn the way of "Beloving" the world in Christ's name. Baptism is a living sacrament of that most basic need: to belong.

When I baptize people, I ask them to share their faith and they share the ancient baptismal creed, "Jesus Christ is Lord." Then I ask the congregation to repeat after me these three phrases of welcome and belonging: "We rejoice in you. We will pray for you. And we will walk with you in the way of Jesus." This is baptism as belonging.

IV.

New Testament scholar Paul Minear counts 114 images of the church in the New Testament.[5] Paul's most frequent image was the "body of Christ." In such a church, he says we are "members of one another" (Rom 12:4-5). The church is not an aggregation of individual members; we are members of one another in the body of Christ.

Paul is anxious to say to the church at Corinth that every member of the body is of equal dignity and worth. In that church, issues of rank, class, and worth had become a point of division, so Paul writes saying that we are all given spiritual gifts, and all are worthy and all are needed. So to those who feel that their gifts are not worthy or needed, he says, "If the foot would say, 'Because I am not a hand, I do not belong to the body,' that would not make it any less a part of the body" (1 Cor 12:15). Yes, you and your gifts belong! And as for those who look down on others' gifts, Paul says, "The eye cannot say to the hand, 'I have no need of you' . . ." (1 Cor 12:21).

All are worthy and all are needed. Paul goes even farther. He says we should give greater honor to those in the body whom the world deems less honorable and lift up those deemed less respectable. Who then may have been deemed less honorable, less respectable? Paul used the analogy of the body to say these are the parts we hide. Gentile converts? Women? Slaves? Those who committed the obvious sins, the public sins, the sins deemed worse than others? Whoever they were, through the years the church has had a problem classifying and ranking members, some worthy and others not. Paul won't let churches off the hook.

For decades in the South, Black church members had to sit in the balconies of white churches. Divorce disqualified many from serving in the church. For centuries, the church has denied the spiritual gifts of women and LGBTQ+ people. Today, more and more churches are rejoicing in the enormous spiritual gifts these people bring. Jesus and Paul would be pleased.

V.

In Galatians, Paul offers this baptismal formula about the revolutionary nature of the body of Christ: "As many of you as were baptized into Christ have clothed yourselves with Christ. There is no longer Jew or Greek, there is no longer slave or free, there is no longer male and female; for all of you are one in Christ Jesus" (Gal 3:27-28). These words reflect Jesus' own life and ministry as he welcomed all people into the kingdom of God and crossed boundaries of race, religion, class, gender, and nation to bring the love of God to everyone. He touched the untouchables and did not turn away from the sick. He ate with tax collectors and sinners, calling them his friends and enjoying their company. He drove the religious folks crazy.

In the kingdom of God and the body of Christ, old creation distinctions still exist, but now they have lost their power to divide. As we follow Jesus and "clothe ourselves with him," we are being transformed. We look around and see the brother/sister kinship of all people. As Paul expressed it, "From now on, therefore, we regard no one from a human point of view . . ." (2 Cor 5:16).

Those revolutionary baptismal words of Paul have often been too much for the church to handle; 2,000 years later we are still running to keep up with Jesus. But inasmuch as we "clothe ourselves with Christ," this is how we live in the community of belonging that is the community of Christ.

VI.

At baptism, those being baptized often wear white robes, and at infant baptism the child wears a white baptismal gown.

The white robe is not a sign of our moral purity or spiritual perfection. It is an emblem of our equality with one another in Christ. But it is even more. At baptism, we put on *Christ*. He is our robe. And as we follow him and put him on, we "are being transformed," as Paul phrased it, "from one degree of glory to another" (2 Cor 3:18).

In the body of Christ, we are learning and experiencing all the meanings of baptism: to follow Jesus and call him Lord, to become the beloved, to turn and enter the kingdom of God, to be washed and forgiven, to experience new birth and the new creation, to receive the Holy Spirit and discover our calling, and to know what it means to belong.

Notes

1. Brian Jay Jones, *Becoming Dr. Seuss: Theodor Geisel and the Making of an American Imagination* (New York: Dutton, 2019), 204. The "seven needs" are (1) a need for security; (2) a need to belong; (3) a need to love and be loved; (4) a need to achieve; (5) a need to know; (6) a need for aesthetic satisfaction; and (7) a need for change.

2. Alister McGrath, *Redemption* (London: SPCK, 2006).

3. John Milton, quoted in Reynolds Price, *A Common Room: Essays, 1954–1987* (New York: Atheneum,1987), 16.

4. Marcus Borg, "What Is a Christian?" November 5, 2013, marcus-jborg.org/posts-by-marcus/what-is-a-christian/. Originally published on Patheos.

5. Paul Sevier Minear, *Images of the Church in the New Testament* (New Testament Library; Louisville: Westminster John Knox Press, 2004).]

Chapter 9

Baptism as Dying and Rising

Baptism signifies dying and rising, both in this life and in the resurrection life to come.

In the mode of baptism called "immersion," we go under the water and out again, a vivid picture of death and rebirth. As part of the baptismal liturgy used by some, as the person is lowered into the water the minister says, "Buried with Christ in baptism," and as the person comes out of the water the minister says, "Raised to walk in newness of life."

This dying and rising is an important dimension of life in Christ. God has resurrection in mind for us here in this life. Something dies so that something is born. An important question to ask often is, "What needs to die so that something may live?"

I.

At Caesarea Philippi Jesus said to his disciples, "If any want to become my followers, let them deny themselves and take up their cross and follow me." Then he added, "For those who want to save their life will lose it, and those who lose their life for my sake, and for the sake of the gospel, will save it" (Mark 8:34-35). Here is the mystery of the gospel: finding comes in losing; losing helps us find.

What does it mean to deny oneself? Does this have something to do with dying and rising? Does it mean to repudiate the self or extinguish the self? No. To deny oneself for the sake of another is a form of love, but that is not the meaning here. The Sufis talk about "dying before you die." It is about letting go of the things that are bringing death so that we might more fully live.

II.

One way to talk about dying and rising is to talk about the denial of the false self—the self we have created and that the world around us has shaped—and the discovery of the true self created by God. The false self is full of compulsions. What the church through the centuries has called the seven deadly sins—pride, sloth, envy, anger, greed, gluttony, and lust, we could call "compulsions of the false self." These are distortions of the true self and distortions of the love by which we were born.

Paul contrasted the "works of the flesh," *sarx*, with the fruit of the Spirit. The works of the flesh as listed are "fornication, impurity, licentiousness, idolatry, sorcery, enmities, strife, jealousy, anger, quarrels, dissensions, factions, envy, drunkenness, carousing, and things like these!" (Gal 5:19-21a). These come from the false self. In contrast, the fruit of the Spirit are these nine: "love, joy, peace, patience, kindness, generosity, faithfulness, gentleness, and self-control" (Gal 5:22-23). We put away some things so that our lives can flourish.

But the false-self/real-self distinction goes deeper—to our spiritual identity. Thomas Merton has been helpful to many as he wrote about the spiritual life as a putting away of the false self so we may discover the true self, the self God has made us to be. The false self, Merton writes, is the "illusory self": "Each of us is shadowed by an illusory person: a false self. . . . We are not very good at recognizing illusions, least of all the ones we cherish about ourself."[1]

The false self is the idealized self, the one we project onto the world and pretend to be. We might call it the "social media self," the one we send out to the world seeking "likes" and approval. But such a self is dangerous to ourselves and others. It takes on a false innocence that hides the wrong we do to ourselves and to other people. It is a self-defeating self.

The time comes, though, when the idol of our perfect idealized self tumbles from the mantle and shatters into a thousand pieces. When this happens, we should thank God for this shattering, for now we can begin to discover the true self. The true self is the one created in the image of God. Merton says it is "hidden in God"; so we can know it only as we enter into God. One can picture the spiritual life as a journey through all the layers of false self down to the true self at the center. Christ is our guide. Merton writes, "The only true joy on earth is to escape from the prison of our own false self, and enter by love into union with the Life Who dwells and sings within the essence of every creature and is the core of our own souls."[2]

The spiritual life is daily dying and rising, dying to the false self and rising to a newer, fuller life.

III.

Now come the resurrections. Robert Furey, a psychotherapist, tells the story of a PhD named Jud. He was successful,

but something vital was lost. After a few sessions, Jud said
to his therapist,

> I have to tell you something I haven't told anyone. . . . I
> don't have my own laugh. . . . I really don't. I laugh like
> other people. . . . When I laugh I can tell whose laugh I
> am using. It's never mine. I think I lost mine sometime
> back. Sometimes I get scared that I've lost it forever.[3]

Jud found his laugh as he began to work among homeless
people. As he ministered to them, they introduced him to
himself, and then came his own unique inimitable laugh.

Wendell Berry wrote a poem, "Manifesto: The Mad
Farmer Liberation Front," whose last line has captured my
spiritual imagination. Early in the poem he says,

> So, friends, every day do something
> that won't compute. Love the Lord.
> Love the world. . .
> Love someone who does not deserve it . . .
> Laugh
> Laughter is immeasurable. Be joyful
> Though you have considered all the facts.

And then this final line: "Practice resurrection."[4]

Followers of Jesus practice resurrection because we
believe that beyond every death comes resurrection. In
April 1998, my dad was close to death in the ICU of a
hospital in Charleston. He had suffered the bursting of
an aneurysm in his aorta and would live only a few more
days. It was the weekend of the Cooper River 10K race. My
brother Jim and I decided to run it in honor of our dad.
We asked the ICU nurse if we could borrow two hospital
gowns, the kind with pastel designs and the opening in the

back. We put them on over our running shorts and ran, ran for life, ran for our dad, ran for life in the face of death. Every day we can find ways to practice resurrection.

Finally, we practice resurrection when we claim joy. Joy is not a subtheme of Scripture. "The joy of the LORD is your strength" (Neh 8:10). When you feel joy, you experience grace. We practice joy because Jesus has bequeathed it to us: "I have said these things to you so that my joy may be in you, and that your joy may be complete" (John 15:11). The poet Mary Oliver writes,

> If you suddenly and unexpectedly feel joy
> don't hesitate. Give in to it . . .
> don't be afraid
> of its plenty. Joy is not meant to be a crumb.[5]

The poet Jack Gilbert urges joy, even amid the wreckage and darkness of our world:

> We must risk delight . . .
> We must have
> the stubbornness to accept our gladness in the ruthless
> furnace of the world.[6]

We practice resurrection when we wage life against all the powers of death in the world. We practice resurrection when we stand with those whose lives are being battered by the systems that bring them death. We are raised up and help others rise.

Baptism is a living sacrament of dying and rising. It is the spiritual practice of letting go of what is killing us and practicing the resurrection that Christ brings.

Notes

1. Thomas Merton, *New Seeds of Contemplation* (New York: New Directions, 2007), 34.

2. Ibid., 25.

3. Robert Furey, *Called by Name* (New York: Crossroad, 1996), 22–28.

4. Wendell Berry, "Manifesto: The Mad Farmer Liberation Front," *The Selected Poems of Wendell Berry* (Washington, DC: Counterpoint, 1998), 87.

5. Mary Oliver, "Don't Hesitate," *Devotions* (New York: Penguin, 2017), 61.

6. Jack Gilbert, "A Brief for the Defense," from his *Refusing Heaven* (New York: Knopf, 2005), and found in Christian Wiman, *Joy: 100 Poems* (New Haven: Yale University Press, 2017), 36.

Chapter 10

Baptism as Resurrection and Eternal Life

Here is why I love to baptize people on Easter morning or Easter eve: baptism is not only a sign of dying and rising in this life; it is also a living sacrament of our resurrection with Christ and the gift of eternal life. As Christ was raised from the dead, so shall we be raised.

For some Christians, the focus on heaven is so great that what happens in this life is of little importance. For other Christians, the focus is on the here and now as the primary arena of living a Christian life, and life in the world to come is of little importance. Some turn away from talk about heaven because the way it is described has so little to do with the kingdom of heaven Jesus talked about. Streets paved with gold, pearly gates, and angels with harps? Mark Twain quipped that if harp playing were all that great, more would be doing it in *this* life.

In this, the last of the chapters on the meanings of baptism, I hope to kindle your hope in eternal life.

I.

It all begins with Christ's resurrection on Easter morning. In his great sermon of resurrection in 1 Corinthians 15, Paul writes, "If for this life only we have hoped in Christ, we are of all people most to be pitied" (15:19). The unusual force of his words suggests that at the church in Corinth, hope in eternal life had been dismissed or at least diminished in importance. Paul is trying to kindle hope in eternal life too! Then he sounds the glad hope of life in the world to come: "But in fact Christ has been raised from the dead, the first fruits of those who have died. For since death came through a human being, the resurrection of the dead has also come through a human being; for as all die in Adam, so all will be made alive in Christ" (15:20-22).

All, all, all, ringing out as all the bells in the world sounding at once. God is opening heaven's gate to all. As Paul says to Timothy, "God our Savior . . . desires everyone to be saved and to come to the knowledge of the truth" (1 Tim 2:3-4). Let us not draw back from this great hope: the final salvation of all.

If your hope grows dim about resurrection and eternal life, go to church on Easter morning and sing with other faithful, hopeful voices, "Christ the Lord is risen today. Alleluia!" In Bach's masterpiece, his *B-Minor Mass*, there is one section named "Credo" where he sets the Nicene Creed to music. In "Et Resurrexit" we thrill to the music of Christ's resurrection. In "Et Expecto" our hearts swell with hope and joyful expectation of our resurrection into eternal life. Sometimes singing the faith helps us believe it with our whole being. The mind descends into the heart and our soul believes. This old hymn helps us believe:

There's a land that is fairer than day,
and by faith we can see it afar,
for the Father waits over the way
to prepare us a dwelling place there.[1]

II.

The two foundational creeds of the Christian faith, the Apostles' Creed and the Nicene Creed, both end with the great hope of eternal life:

I believe . . . in the resurrection of the body; and in life everlasting. (Apostles' Creed)

We look forward to the resurrection of the dead, and the life of the world to come. (Nicene Creed)

Our resurrection is our passage to the world to come. It is part of the great hope of the Christian faith.

III.

What will life be like in the heaven of the world to come? It will be the Final Healing. The medieval mystic Julian of Norwich was given visions from God that she called "Showings." In one, she was given this vision of the world to come:

All shall be well
and all shall be well
and all manner of thing shall be well.[2]

That she was given such a vision during the Black Death that swept Europe in the fourteenth century makes her words even more poignant.

Life in the world to come will be the Great Home-coming where we will dwell with God and God will dwell with us. Reunion and reconciliation will be won. It will be the Final Rejoicing, where, as J. R. R. Tolkien expressed it, there will be "Joy, joy, beyond the walls of this world."[3] It will be wonderful beyond our imagining. As Paul said, "no eye has seen, nor ear heard, nor the human heart conceived, what God has prepared for those who love him" (1 Cor 2:9).

A year or so ago I was preparing a sermon on "Heaven and Eternal Life." I told my mother, who was then nine-ty-four, about the sermon and asked her what she thought of heaven. She said, with a lifetime of Christian teaching within her, "I don't know, but it will be good." Simplicity beyond complexity. Good beyond what we can think or imagine.

Theologian Christopher Morse says that when Chris-tians think about heaven, they too often get hung up on *chronology* (when will it happen?), *geography* (where is it, and what will it look like?), and *census* (who will be there?).[4] We can get stuck in the literalness of thoughts and ideas about heaven and lose the poetry of our hope—our language that points to the ineffable mystery of life in the eternal presence of God.

We have been given glimpses of the world to come, like those given to Julian of Norwich. John on the isle of Patmos was given this glimpse: "After this I looked, and there was a great multitude that no one could count, from every nation, from all tribes and people and languages, standing before the throne and before the Lamb" (Rev 7:9). Beauty beyond chronology, geography, and census.

John Donne, poet and preacher at St. Paul's Cathedral in London, was given visions. He had been struck with an illness that he thought would end his life. While ill, he wrote a set of essays called *Devotions Upon Emergent Conditions*. In Meditation 17 he offers this vision of the world to come:

> All mankind is of one Author, and is of one volume. When one man dies, one chapter is not torn out of the book, but translated into a better language, and every chapter must be translated. . . . God's hand is in every translation. And his hand shall bind up all our scattered leaves again, for that Library where every book shall be open to one another.[5]

In the mystery of the resurrection, "we will all be changed" (1 Cor 15:51). This is the Easter good news of God in Christ. We will see one another with transformed faces.

Some may balk at the talk of heaven with all its speculation and argumentation over chronology, geography, and census, but our resurrection hope persists. Heaven's hope is planted in us because of our spiritual longing for home, home with God, with others, and with our own true selves. As Scripture says, "The eternal God is your dwelling place, and underneath are the everlasting arms" (Deut 33:27, ESV).

Frederick Buechner's mother was not religious, so it came as shock one day when out of the blue she asked him, "Do you really believe anything *happens* after you die?" Caught off guard, all he could say was, "Yes, I believe something happens." But he knew he wanted to say more, so he wrote her a letter. Here is how he described it:

I wrote her I believe that what happens when you die is that, in ways I knew no more about than she did, you are given your life back again, and I said that there are three reasons why I believed it. First, I wrote her, I believed it because, if I were God and loved the people I created and wanted them to become at last the best they had it in them to be, I couldn't imagine consigning them to oblivion when their time came with the job, under the best of circumstances only a fraction done. Second, I said, I believed it apart from any religious considerations, because I had a hunch it was true. I intuited it. I said that if the victim and victimizers, the wise and the foolish, the good-hearted and heartless, all end up alike in the grave and that is the end of it, then life would be like a black comedy, and to me, even at its worst, life doesn't *feel* like a black comedy. It feels like a mystery. And lastly, I wrote her, I believe that what happens to us after we die is that we aren't dead forever because Jesus said so.[6]

Buechner didn't know how his mother would take his invoking Jesus' name and authority and how she would respond to his letter. He asked her later and she said it made her cry.

Why do we cry or get lumps in our throats when we think about the world to come or sing about it in the hymns of our faith? Is it the thought that all shall be well, that the best is not at the mercy of the worst, that death has not the final word but life does, that hate is not the final word but love is? It is so for me, as with a lump in my throat the size of Texas I look forward to the joy beyond the walls of this world. We may not need such words this day, but one day we may, and such hope will be given.

In the ancient church, baptismal candidates would stand in the river at dawn on Easter. They would turn to the darkened west and renounce the powers of darkness. Then they would turn to the east toward the dawning sun and declare, "Jesus Christ is Lord!" In this practice, all the meanings of baptism find their triumphant end: resurrection and eternal life.

Easter happened, and it happens still. Poet Gerard Manley Hopkins voices our daily hope:

> Let him easter in us, be a dayspring to the dimness of us,
> be a crimson-cresseted east
> More brightening [us] . . . as his reign rolls . . . .[7]

Yes, may Christ easter in us until the day of our final eastering. Let the alleluias begin.

Notes

1. "In the Sweet By-and-By," words by S. Fillmore Bennett, music by J. P. Webster, 1868.

2. This widely quoted line by Julian of Norwich is adapted into modern English by the author. The original English version is found in *Revelations of Divine Love* (London: Methuen, 1950), 56.

3. J. R. R. Tolkien, as cited in Frederick Buechner, *Telling the Truth: The Gospel as Tragedy, Comedy, and Fairy Tale* (New York: Harper & Row, 1977), 81.

4. Christopher Morse, *The Difference Heaven Makes: Rehearsing the Gospel as News* (London: T&T Clarke, 2010).

5. John Donne, "Meditation 17," *Devotions Upon Emergent Occasions* (New York: Oxford University Press, 1987), 86. Rendered here in my modern English version.

6. Frederick Buechner, *The Eyes of the Heart* (New York: Harper San Francisco, 1999), 14–16.

7. Gerard Manley Hopkins, "The Wreck of the Deutschland," *The Poems of Gerard Manley Hopkins* (Oxford: Oxford University Press, 1970), 63.

Chapter 11

Pastoral Reflections on the Theology and Practice of Baptism

I have written this book as a form of pastoral theology. I write as a minister in the "free-church" tradition, which means I have the freedom—for better and for worse—to practice baptism in the local congregation, drawing upon the full range of liturgical practices in the church through the centuries. Such liturgical and theological improvisations can have weaknesses and error, but I have sought to be faithful to the deepest meanings of the practice of baptism. I now offer some general reflections in the hope of stirring conversation that can enrich the practice of baptism in the church today.

I.

British Baptist theologian Paul Fiddes writes of going to preach at an ecumenical congregation, Christ the Cornerstone in Milton Keynes, England, which offered its congregation both infant baptism and believer's baptism. The church had a combination of a font to be used for infant baptism and a baptistry to be used for believer's baptism. Water constantly flowed from the font to the baptistry and then back again from the baptistry to the font. This powerful image captures what this chapter is all about. Baptism is the culmination of a journey into faith from infancy onward, marked by moments where grace and faith come together in the life of the child of God.

II.

The ecumenical movement, begun over one hundred years ago, sought to foster unity in Christ's deeply divided church, the church Christ prayed and still prays might be united as one. This chapter is written in that spirit, with care for the unity of the church. The sacraments of baptism and the Eucharist have been theological battlegrounds through the centuries. The ecumenical movement has sponsored conversations that seek to make baptism and the Eucharist more a sign of unity than division. Its proponents have explored the meaning of what Paul called "one baptism": "There is one body and one Spirit . . . one hope . . . one Lord, one faith, one baptism, one God and Father of all, who is above all and through all and in all" (Eph 4:4-6). Their goal has been to develop a "common baptism" shared by all.

Keith Watkins reports what he calls "a new consensus" on baptism in these ecumenical discussions.[1] A key document of this developing consensus is *Baptism, Eucharist and Ministry.*[2] Here are five places of growing consensus:

One, *the liturgical standard for baptism is the full set of actions that Western churches have split into separate rites and ceremonies.* These are (1) the presentation of the candidate; (2) the profession of faith; (3) the baptism; (4) the laying on of hands; and (5) the welcome and the sharing in Communion, or Eucharist.

Two, *the baptism of people who can speak for themselves is the theological norm.* New Testament scholars and theologians have increasingly supported this position.[3]

Three, *other rites and ceremonies for early childhood are being given greater prominence*; for example, infant and child dedication ceremonies that combine the blessing of the child and the dedication of the parents and congregation.

Four, the *decisive character of baptism for the scheme of redemption is being reclaimed*; for example, participation in Christ's death and resurrection, conversion, pardoning and cleansing, the gift of the Holy Spirit, incorporation into the body of Christ, and entrance into the kingdom of God. This book has sought to illuminate and expand on these, and more, dimensions of redemption in baptism.

Five, *although baptism is done only once, the renewal of baptismal vows can and needs to occur repeatedly.* The theological issue of whether or not a "second baptism" is permissible is a continuing place of division. The way forward requires an avoidance of positions that call infant baptism null and void on the one hand and call "re-baptism" a heresy on the other. There has been too much acrimony and spilling of blood through the centuries over baptism.

As a Baptist pastor, I believe "believer's baptism" churches should welcome all who come from "infant baptism" churches without requiring a "second baptism." Paul Fiddes writes, "Baptists should in fact be quite willing to recognize that there are elements of both faith and divine grace in the act which is called infant baptism."[4] I also believe—and will discuss below—that there are occasions when a second baptism is pastorally and spiritually appropriate. But I proceed carefully here.

Fiddes expresses concern about elements of the ecumenical pursuit of "common baptism." Instead, he offers as a way forward an acknowledgment of a "common process" towards faith, into faith, and within faith of which baptism is the central expression—and including at some point the faith commitment of the person.[5] We are talking about a common journey toward faith that honors those sacred moments where grace and faith meet and are marked by sacramental action.

III.

Let's focus first on the child in the church. In infant baptism, faith and grace are at work: the gracious presence of God and the faith of the parents and congregation. The whole journey into faith is an interplay of grace and faith.[6]

More and more churches in other traditions are offering a service of child dedication, where the blessing of the child and the dedication of the family and church are combined. Early Baptists called this ceremony "the devotion of children," a beautiful phrase. It shows God's devotion to the child and the devotion of the parents and the congregation. The 1979 Episcopal *Book of Common Prayer* includes this prayer of blessing in a service at the birth or adoption of a child:

> O God, you have taught us through your blessed Son that whoever receives a little child in the name of Christ receives Christ himself: We give you thanks for the blessing you have bestowed upon this family in giving them a child. Confirm their joy by a lively sense of your presence with them and give them calm strength and

patient wisdom as they seek to bring this child to love all that is true and noble, just and pure, lovable and gracious, excellent and desirable, following the example of our Lord and Savior, Jesus Christ. *Amen.*[7]

In my ministry I have offered a service of child dedication in Sunday worship for children and parents, one at a time, as infants come into the world or as children and their parents become members of the church. After an opening prayer of thanksgiving and dedication and a litany by the whole congregation, I carry the child (or walk the child) into the congregation, introducing the child and saying words of welcome and blessing to the child. These services have become sacred moments for the congregation as well as for the family. They experience delight in the child, and the child experiences God's delight in them. As I speak God's "original blessing" to the child, they experience vicariously their own original blessing, a moment of grace to many of them who, growing up, heard about "original sin" much more than "original blessing."

As the child begins a sacred journey toward faith, the church provides worship, teaching, and nurture. John Westerhoff has five guidelines about such nurture:

1. We need to tell and retell the biblical story—the stories of the faith together—so it becomes our common story.
2. We need to celebrate our faith and our lives and participate in liturgy and eucharist together.
3. We need to pray together.
4. We need to listen and talk to each other about our experiences and relationship to God.
5. We need to perform faithful acts of service and witness together.[8]

In his book *The Spiritual Life of Children*, Harvard professor of psychology and medical humanities Robert Coles says that children "are soulful in ways they themselves reveal."[9] Parents and congregations are called to be attentive to their children so that they can see and hear them as they reveal their soulfulness.

As Westerhoff recommends, one of the ways we nurture our children in the faith is to bring them to worship. My own thoughts are that as soon as it is spiritually and developmentally appropriate, children should be welcomed to worship. The amount of time they spend in worship can correspond to their age. Sitting with their family in worship and singing hymns, listening to their family pray, and hearing Scripture can provide rich spiritual nurture. As Jesus said, "Let the children come unto me."

The issue of when children should be invited to the Lord's Table is a most debated one. In the Roman Catholic church, "first communion" is celebrated in middle childhood. The offering of the sacrament is accompanied by spiritual instruction appropriate for that age. Grace and faith meet in that time of sacramental significance.

In believer's baptism churches, the common practice is to withhold the Table until the person is baptized. More of these churches are opening the Table to children and young people before baptism. It corresponds to the spiritual and emotional need of the child to belong. It offers the prevenient grace of God as God's grace and the faith of the child meet. John Wesley served the Eucharist to unbaptized, unchurched people because he believed the Eucharist was a "converting sacrament." In the young person's journey toward faith, into faith, and within faith, such sacred actions can correspond to the measure of faith given at that time in their lives. Here are some guidelines to consider: (1) the child should express spiritual interest in taking Communion; (2) the parents should want this for their child; (3) the church should welcome the child's participation.

IV.

As a pastor, I have sought to incorporate as much of the "ecumenical consensus" regarding baptismal theology as was appropriate for the congregations I have served. Here are some of the reflections that have shaped those efforts.

1. I sought an acknowledgment of the meaning of "one baptism" by not requiring a "re-baptism" for those who had been baptized as infants for membership in the church. Over the past fifty years, a number of Baptist churches have been "dis-fellowshipped" by local Baptist associations for this practice, sometimes called "open baptism." Ecumenical advance is never easy.

2. The normal practice in Baptist churches has been to expect and encourage young people to be baptized when they feel the Spirit leading them to follow Jesus. Individual congregations have set the expectation of when a person should be baptized, most often from middle childhood to teenage years.

At Myers Park Baptist Church in Charlotte, the American Baptist church I served, we offered eighth graders a yearlong discipleship class, where they learned about Christian and Baptist beliefs to prepare them for baptism. The children visited other congregations for worship, including non-Christian congregations. I would teach them the meanings of baptism during a retreat in the spring, after which they would decide whether or not to be baptized at that time. We offered freedom for them to say yes or no, and we honored all decisions. If a young person had been baptized as an infant, we did not require a second baptism. If they wished to be baptized by immersion with their peers as a confirmation of their original baptism, we did so with clear words spoken about the meaning of the person's baptism. If they wished to be "confirmed" on that day without baptism, I laid hands on them in the service.

In believer's baptism churches, there has been discussion about when a young person is old enough to be baptized. What is the "age of accountability"? James McClendon, in his "baptist" (lowercase "b") systematic theology, answered, "When a young person is old enough to say 'no' to parents, peers and culture."[10] For that, the teenage years usually suffice! In some Baptist churches, children, in my estimation, have been encouraged to be baptized at too young an age—and they didn't have the benefit of a confirmation class as most do in infant baptism churches.

Reformed theologian Robert Jenson has argued persuasively for a return to the ancient practice of a "cate- chumenate," when an extended time for catechism is given to those preparing for baptism.[11] The church might offer a class annually or biannually for people of all ages to prepare for baptism. Such a class would be especially appropriate for the season of Lent in preparation for baptism at Easter.

3. I have offered baptismal preparation to anyone seeking to be baptized. I have also offered a service of baptism at the Christmas and Easter holy days, usually on Christmas Eve, at an Easter vigil, or during the Easter Sunday morning service. Baptism in these two holy seasons provides a surplus of meaning for the person being baptized. Also, to be baptized in these moments of the Christian

year gives them a special time each year to remember their baptism.

4. The Lent-to-Easter cycle of days offers the most powerful context as a season of baptismal preparation and baptismal renewal as we remember our baptismal vows. The whole season can teach the meanings of baptism through worship, preaching, small groups, and baptismal preparation classes.

5. Services of baptism in worship should include a meditation on the meaning of baptism, the presentation of the candidate, the confession of faith in Jesus Christ as Lord, the baptism, the response of the congregation in a litany of thanksgiving and dedication, the laying on of hands, and shared Communion. The gathering together of these elements returns us to the ancient practices of the church.

6. I now return to the theologically and spiritually sensitive question of a "second baptism." Is a "rebaptism" or "second baptism" ever appropriate spiritually? I offer a careful and considered *yes*, but only in specific circumstances.

Some call these instances "baptismal repair," meaning there has been an "impaired baptism." The Christian church has struggled with such issues through the centuries.[12] In an "impaired baptism," a person may have been baptized under coercion and knows it was not a freely chosen baptism. The person may have been baptized while being sexually abused. Such people cannot "remember their baptism and be thankful." A second baptism can be the occasion of spiritual healing and great joy. All such decisions must be considered in the context of careful pastoral care and pastoral wisdom.

A public call for "re-baptism" for evangelistic purposes is not appropriate and sometimes does spiritual damage by creating salvation anxiety in the listeners. Questions like "Do you remember exactly the day you were saved?" are voiced, and if the answer is "no," the "solution" is given: "Then you need to be baptized again."

V.

I wrote this chapter seeking to honor the sacramental nature of baptism as we work together toward an ecumenical consensus on baptism for the sake of the unity of the church. This process constitutes what Paul called "knowing in part" (1 Cor 13:9). I hope these reflections will stir conversation that enriches the meaning of baptism. The absence of such conversation has led to impoverishment of the meaning of baptism, and some churches no longer require it for church membership.

Baptism is the central event in a person's journey toward faith, into faith, and within faith. The church should give central meaning to this event in the sacred journey of salvation—no matter when baptism occurs in the person's life. Other rites and ceremonies mark the weaving of grace and faith in a person's life, and the church should give richness to such times, but the central sacrament is baptism. Now we move to the meaning of "baptism as sacrament."

Notes

1. Keith Watkins, *The Great Thanksgiving* (St. Louis: Chalice, 1995), 159–64.

2. *Baptism, Eucharist and Ministry*, Faith and Order Paper 111 (Geneva: World Council of Churches, 1982).

3. Paul Fiddes, *Tracks and Traces: Baptist Identity in Church and Theology* (Eugene: Wipf and Stock, 2003), 119.

4. Ibid.

5. Ibid., 140–43.

6. Ibid., 145.

7. The Episcopal Church, *The Book of Common Prayer* (New York: Seabury, 1979), 443.

8. John H. Westerhoff III, *Bringing Up Children in the Christian Faith* (Minneapolis: Winston Press, 1980), 36. See also his foreword to Gretchen Wolff Pritchard's *Offering the Gospel to Children* (Boston: Cowley Publications, 1992), xi–xii.

9. Robert Coles, *The Spiritual Life of Children* (Boston: Houghton Mifflin, 1990), xviii.

10. James Wm. McClendon Jr., *Doctrine*, vol. 2 of Systematic Theology (Nashville: Abingdon, 1994), 394.

11. Robert W. Jenson, "Catechesis for Our Time," in *Marks of the Body of Christ*, ed. Carl E. Braaten and Robert W. Jenson (Grand Rapids: Eerdmans, 1999), 137–49.

12. McClendon, *Doctrine*, 395–96.

Chapter 12

Baptism as Sacrament: A Meeting Place with God

While the word "sacrament" has been used to describe baptism in Christian churches through the centuries, most Baptists today have rejected it, preferring the word "ordinance," that is, something we do in obedience to the command of Christ. Out of an anti-Catholic bias and rejecting what they call the "magical" element in sacraments, Baptists have reduced baptism to our action alone and not God's action as well. Early Baptists, however, used the word "sacrament" because it was to them a "means of grace."

Baptism is a sacrament because it is a "meeting place" between God and the one being baptized. One might rightly say that there are meeting places everywhere and that there are many sacramental moments. But the church has chosen to offer baptism as a sure and momentous meeting place. God has promised to meet us there.

James McClendon prefers the word "sign" to the words "ordinance" or "sacrament." Baptism, he writes, is one of the "Remembering Signs" of salvation. It is an "acted-sign" that involves both word and action. Moreover, it is an "effectual sign" that points us toward its sacramental character. More is happening at baptism than a person's following the command of Christ. There is a "double agency" at work: God's agency and the agency of the baptized person. There is a "triple agency" too, he writes, for the church is also acting.[1]

An oft-used Protestant definition of a sacrament is that it is "an outward and visible sign of an inward and invisible grace." Grace and faith are entwined in baptism. To paraphrase a psalm, grace and faith kiss (see Psalm 85:10).

Paul Fiddes calls baptism a sacrament because it is, in his words, "a meeting place" with God, a "rendezvous with God."[2] George Beasley-Murray describes baptism as a "trysting-place," a place of faithfulness and love, God's and ours.[3] Therefore baptism is a relational act and a relational event. God and Christ are present with us there.

I like the phrase "meeting place." God has promised to meet us at the Pool as at the Table. The Celtic Christians use the phrase "thin place" to describe when and where the veil between heaven and earth becomes so thin that we experience heaven and earth as one. Baptism is a "thin place." God comes to meet us; we come to meet God. The Pool is a place of meeting.

Here are some of my experiences of sacramental meeting places with God in baptism. At Broadway Baptist Church, we created a weekly Agape Meal for the unhoused community of Fort Worth, Texas. They walked from north, east, south, and west, nearly two hundred of them, to get to the 5:30 meal. We served the meal family-style, with our church members and our guests around the tables together. After the meal, we invited them to stay for worship. About half of them stayed. Other churches sometimes require their guests to go to worship or teaching before receiving a meal. One homeless man said to me, "Thanks for giving us our freedom of religion!"

After the worship time, we invited any who wanted Communion to move to the adjoining chapel. About fifteen to twenty would come. For some, tears flowed down their faces as they took Communion. When you lose your house, you lose your church too—and the sacraments of the church. Some had thought they would never receive Communion again.

Once a year, I offered baptism to the congregation of unhoused neighbors and would announce it weeks in advance so they could ponder their decision. Once such night, we left the chapel after Communion and moved into the sanctuary. The baptismal pool was behind the choir loft. I took the baptismal candidates to be robed for the baptism, and the members and guests sat in the choir loft so they could see close up. As each person came up out of the water, those witnessing the baptism cheered. Then we sang "Amazing Grace." One night I baptized a middle-aged Hispanic man named Moses. As he came up out of the water, he whispered to me, "I am now ready to die."

A young adult woman in one of my churches had suffered sexual abuse from a family member years before. She asked for a second baptism as a sacred action of a new beginning, a baptism not impaired by the memories of abuse that haunted her first one. She felt that years of shame and guilt were now being washed away. The cleansing water of baptism was the sign of a new life. As she left the pool, she beamed.

An older woman was a member of Crescent Hill Baptist Church in Louisville. She now lived about forty miles away, in the medical unit of her senior care facility. She called and asked that I baptize her. She had grown up at Crescent Hill Baptist but had not been baptized like most of her adolescent peers because she had physical deformities and felt too embarrassed about her body to do so. We visited and then, a few days later, I returned and baptized her by affusion in her bed, gently pouring a little water on her head. She was joyous. As I was leaving, she pointed out to me the clear bottle of blue liquid morphine above her bed, which was dripping into her body for pain relief. She said to me, "That's the most beautiful shade of blue I've ever seen!" I felt like it was a holy moment, a meeting place with God. God was there, she was there, and I was graciously asked to be there.

A brilliant young adult, now a professor of religion, started attending Myers Park Baptist Church. He told me privately that he was coming to church to open himself to the "possibility of God" and the possibility of believing. A year or so later, he asked to be baptized. We went to the lake accompanied by a community of friends. Before the baptism, he asked if he could say a few words in the water before he was immersed. I said, "Of course." We stood there together, the water sparkling with the sun. Here were his words, the words of Jesus:

Come to me, all who are weary and heavy laden, and I will give you rest. Take my yoke upon you, and learn from me; for I am gentle and lowly in heart, and you

will find rest for your souls. For my yoke is easy, and my
burden is light. (Matt 11:28-30)

This Voice had led him to the water, and Christ was present
with him there. It was a thin place. Heaven and earth had
met.

I was helping lead a choir retreat at the beach. On
the last day of the retreat, I had planned a ceremony of
baptismal renewal. I preached on the baptism of the Ethiopian eunuch by Philip in Acts 8. I then offered the invitation
to proceed to the ocean and pair up. The attendees were to
fill their cupped hands with sea water and pour it over the
head of the other person as they said, "Jesus Christ is Lord."

As we began to walk out of the room toward the ocean,
Damien, a young Polish man who had recently immigrated
to the US and who had joined the choir, came up to me.
Echoing the eunuch's words, he said, "Here is water. Will
you baptize me today?" "Yes," I said, and we went into the
ocean where it was about three feet deep. Suddenly, shark
fins rose out of the water about twenty yards away. We
exited the ocean in a less dignified way than we had entered.
Then someone saw a hotel pool next to the beach. It had
a "lazy river" of flowing water around the pool. We went
there. The choir followed and surrounded us. Above on
three sides, people from several floors of balconies watched
the baptism. For some of them, it was no doubt the first
time they had seen a baptism. As Damien came out of the
water, the choir sang "Amazing Grace." The sun sparkled
on the water. Our makeshift baptism became a sacramental
meeting place.

At baptism, in this meeting place with God, it is all
there, all the meanings and more: following Jesus, being
the beloved, naming Jesus Lord, turning and entering the

kingdom, washing, new birth and new creation, belonging
to a family of faith, anointing, Holy Spirit and calling,
dying and rising, and resurrection and eternal life.

"As John Calvin says," Will Willimon writes, "God
remembers that we are creatures, and so the Creator loves
us in ways we can understand—in bread and wine and
water."[4] God is loving us in the waters of baptism. Now
and always.

Notes

1. James Wm. McClendon, *Doctrine*, vol. 2 of Systematic Theology
(Nashville: Abingdon, 1994), 382–97.

2. Paul Fiddes, *Tracks and Traces: Baptist Identity in Church and Theology*
(Eugene: Wipf and Stock, 2003), 128.

3. George Beasley-Murray, *Baptism in the New Testament* (London:
Macmillan & Co., 1962), 305.

4. William H. Willimon, *A Guide to Preaching and Leading Worship*
(Louisville: Westminster Press, 1984), 13.

Chapter 13

Liturgies and Worship Services for Baptism and Baptismal Renewal

I have baptized people in church baptistries, rivers, lakes, by bedsides, in backyard swimming pools, and, yes, in the "lazy river" of a beachfront hotel. Words, liturgies, and prayers have varied from simple to formal, low church to high church to no church. Music has been provided by grand pipe organs, old family pianos, and through instruments of many kinds. The Holy is everywhere.

In this final chapter, I offer a sample of liturgies and orders of worship I have used through the years. There have been many more. These are provided for your reflection, guidance, and perhaps adaption in your own congregational settings.

The Dedication of Children

The dedication of infants and children in worship has been called "A Service of Child Dedication" or "A Service of Family Dedication." The service also involves the dedication of the congregation.

My practice was to dedicate infants and children one family at a time, as the child was born or as a family brought children with them as they joined the church. This sacred practice has increased the bond between the child, the family, and the congregation. Here is the "Service of Family Dedication" I used at Myers Park Baptist Church.

THE SERVICE OF FAMILY DEDICATION

People: Mighty God, by your love we are given children through the miracle of birth. We give you thanks. May we greet each new son and daughter with joy and surround them with faith, so they may know who you are and want to be your disciples.

Never let us neglect children, but help us to delight in them, showing them the welcome you have shown us all through Jesus Christ our Lord. Amen.

Leader: In presenting your child to God, do you promise in dependence upon God's grace and with the help of the church to teach her the gifts and claims of the Christian faith, and by prayer, word, and example to bring her up in the nurture, discipline, and instruction of the Lord?

Parents: We do.

Leader: Brothers and sisters of the household of faith, I commend to you this family. Will you covenant to stand with them in the nurture of this child? Will you stay constant in success and failure? Will you do all in your power to make this church a spiritual home for them, lending them the support of your prayers and your example?

People: With God's help we will so seek to follow Christ ourselves that this family will be strengthened and confirmed in their resolve, and that this child, surrounded by steadfast love, may be nurtured in the faith and be strengthened in the way that leads to life.

The Prayer of Family Dedication
God of grace, Perfect Parent of us all, we pray for these parents, and for all parents and for all who parent in the Lord. Help them to know you, to love with your love, to teach with your truth, and to tell the story of Jesus to their children so that your word may be heard. Bless this child. Guard her safely through injury and illness that she may live the promises you give. And keep us, with this child and with all children ready to listen and to love, even as in Jesus Christ you have loved us, your grown-up children. In whose name we pray. Amen.

I would then carry the child or walk with the child into the congregation, as I have written about above.

A Service of Baptism for Easter Morning Worship

The Call to Worship
The Organ Voluntary
The Easter Gospel Lesson (from one of the Gospels)
The Choral Introit
The Processional Hymn
The Invocation
The Organ Interlude

The Service of Baptism
    The Baptismal Vows
    Candidate: "Jesus Christ is Lord."

Minister: Hear the pledge of your family of faith

Congregation: We rejoice with you. We will pray for you. And we will walk with you in the way of Jesus.

A Service of Baptismal Renewal

Leader: For the promise is to you and to your children and to all that are far off, every one called by God to God (Acts 2:39). I invite you to the renewal of your baptismal vows.

People: In this place and in the name of the Father, of the Son, and of the Holy Spirit, I, _____, this day renew my vows of baptism, believing in the promises of God who raised Jesus from the grave. Jesus Christ is Lord.

The Choral Anthem
The Second Lesson
The Hymn of Easter
The Sermon
The Hymn of Response
The Morning Offertory
The Doxology

The Easter Proclamation
People: This is the good news which we received, in which we stand, and by which we are saved: that Christ

died for our sins according to the Scriptures, that he was buried, that he was raised on the third day; that he appeared to Peter, then to the twelve and to many faithful witnesses. *(from 1 Corinthians 15:1-6)*

The Choral Response ("Hallelujah," Handel or Beethoven)
The Organ Dismissal

An Easter Vigil Service with Baptism and the Renewal of Baptismal Vows

(This formal service can be adapted for a less liturgical worship.)

The Great Vigil of Easter—Holy Saturday, nine o'clock in the evening

The Community Gathers Before God
The Chiming of the Hour

The Kindling of the New Fire
Leader: The Lord be with you.

People: And with your spirit.

Leader: Let us pray. Eternal God, in Jesus Christ you have given the light of life to all the world. Bless the lighting of this new fire that we may shine with the brightness of Christ's rising. Through Jesus Christ our Lord.

People: Amen.

Cantor: *(sung)* The Light of Christ.

People: *(sung)* **Thanks be to God.**

The Lighting of the Paschal Candle
Leader: The light of Christ rises in glory, overcoming the darkness of sin.

Cantor: *(sung)* The Light of Christ.

People: *(sung)* **Thanks be to God.**

The Lighting of the Congregational Candles
Leader: Jesus Christ is the Light of the World.

People: A light no darkness can extinguish.

Cantor: *(sung)* The Light of Christ.

People: (sung) Thanks be to God.

The Procession into the Church
"The Exultet," *Plainsong*

The Service of the Word
The First Reading: *The Creation of Humanity*, Genesis 1:1, 26-31

Leader: The word of God.
People: Thanks be to God.

The Psalm Motet (Psalm 33:1-3)
"Exsultate, justi, in Domino" (Lodovico da Viadana, c. 1560–1627), The Motet Choir

The Collect

Almighty God, who wonderfully created, yet more wonderfully restored, the dignity of human nature, grant that we may share the divine life of the one who came to share our humanity: Jesus Christ, our Redeemer. Amen.

The Second Reading: *Noah and the Flood*, Genesis 6:17-22; 9:8-17

Leader: The Word of God.

People: Thanks be to God.

The Collect

Almighty God, you have placed in the skies the sign of your covenant with all living things: Grant that we, who are saved through water and the Spirit, may worthily offer to you our sacrifice of thanksgiving through Jesus Christ our Lord. Amen.

The Third Reading: *Abraham and Sarah's Faithfulness*, Genesis 12:1-4

Leader: The Word of God.

People: Thanks be to God.

The Hymn for Response: "The God of Abraham Praise" (Leoni), Number 61

The Collect

Gracious God of all believers, through Sarah's and Abraham's trustful obedience you made known your covenant love to our ancestors and to us. By the grace of Christ's trustful obedience, even unto death, fulfill in your church and in all creation your promise of a new covenant, written not on tablets of stone but on the tablets of human hearts, through Jesus Christ our Savior. Amen.

The Fourth Reading: *Israel's Deliverance at the Red Sea*, Exodus 14:10-29, 21-23

Leader: The Word of God.

People: Thanks be to God.

The Canticle of Moses and Miriam: "Canticle of Moses" (John Karl Hirten, 1995), The Motet Choir

The Collect
God our Savior, even today we see the wonders of the miracles you worked long ago. You once saved a single nation from slavery, and now you offer that salvation to all through the grace of baptism. May all the peoples of the world become true daughters and sons of Abraham and Sarah and be made worthy of the heritage of Israel, through Jesus Christ, our Advocate. Amen.

The Fifth Reading: *Salvation Offered Freely to All*, Isaiah 55:1-11

Leader: The Word of God.

People: Thanks be to God.

The Psalm Motet: "Sicut cervus" (Giovanni Palestrina), The Motet Choir

The Sixth Reading: *The Baptism of Jesus*, Mark 1:9-11

The Service of Baptism
The Baptismal Vow
Candidate: Jesus Christ is Lord.

Leader: Hear now the pledge of the family of faith.

People: We rejoice with you. We will pray for you. We will walk with you in the way of Jesus.

The Seventh Reading: *Dying and Rising with Christ*, Romans 6:3-11

The Hymn of Baptism: "We Know that Christ is Raised" (Engelberg)

The Reaffirmation of Baptismal Vows
Leader: Brothers and Sisters, let us reaffirm the salvation given us in Christ and symbolized in baptism. Do you renounce the dark forces of evil which defy God's righteousness and love?

People: I renounce them.

Leader: Do you turn to Jesus and follow him as Lord and Savior?

People: I do.

Leader: For the promise is to you and to your children and to all that are far off, every one called by God to God (Acts 2:39). I invite you to the renewal for baptismal vows.

People: In this place and in the name of the Father, of the Son, and of the Holy Spirit, I, this day, renew my vows of baptism, believing in the promises of God who raised Jesus from the grave. Jesus Christ is Lord.

The Joyful Feast of the People of God
The Easter Gospel Is Proclaimed: John 20:1-10

Leader: The Gospel of our Lord.

People: Thanks be to God.

The Voluntary at the Offertory: "Allegro in e minor" (Johann Sebastian Bach, 1685–1750)

The Prayer of Thanksgiving
The Lord's Prayer
The Sharing of the Bread and Cup

The Prayer after Communion
People: Lord, we bless you and praise you for nourishing us with the Easter feast of redemption. Fill us with your Spirit and make us living signs of your love. Amen.

The Closing Hymn: "O Sons and Daughters, Let us Sing" (*O filii et filiae*)

A Blessing
The Postlude

A Christmas Eve Service of Lessons and Carols with Baptism

Instrumental Carols
Darkness
Lighting of the Christ Candle
Processional Hymn: "Once in Royal David's City" (Irby)
Greeting and Prayer

A Service of Baptism
The Baptismal Vow
Candidate: Jesus Christ is Lord!

Leader: Hear now the pledge of your family of faith.

Congregation: We rejoice with you. We will pray for you. And we will walk with you in the way of Jesus.

Hymn: "Of the Father's Love Begotten" (Divinium Mysterium)

The First Lesson: Genesis 3:8-15
God announces in the Garden of Eden that the offspring of woman shall strike the serpent's head.

Carol: "Adam Lay Ybounden" (Warlock)

The Second Lesson: Isaiah 9:2, 6-7
Christ's birth and kingdom are foretold by Isaiah.

Carol: "The Truth from Above

The Third Lesson: Micah 5:1-4
The prophet Micah foretells the glory of Bethlehem.

Carol: "O Little Town of Bethlehem" (St. Louis)

The Fourth Lesson: Luke 1:26-35, 38

Carol: "Gabriel's Message"

The Fifth Lesson: Matthew 1:18-23
Matthew tells of the birth of Jesus.

Carol: "Infant Holy, Infant Lowly" (*W Zlobie Lezy*)

The Sixth Lesson: Luke 2:1-7

Carol: "The First Nowell the Angel Did Say" (The First Nowell)

Darkness

The Seventh Lesson: John 1:1-14
John unfolds the mystery of the incarnation.

The Lighting of the Candles from the Christ Candle

Carol: "Silent Night"

The Blessing

Hymn: "O Come All Ye Faithful"

The Postlude

Of the Words Spoken at Baptism

As each person comes into the water, I place my hand on their shoulder and introduce them to the congregation. I speak a few words about the meaning of baptism, sometimes emphasizing one of the meanings that most affected the candidate. I often tell about Jesus' baptism and the words God spoke to him: "You are my son, the beloved, in whom I am well pleased," and I say that I hope they can hear God saying the same to them at this moment of baptism.

I invite the candidate to share their faith in the baptismal vow and then to say "Jesus Christ is Lord." The congregation offers their response as noted above in the liturgies.

I then baptize the candidate with the words, "Upon your profession of faith in Jesus as Lord, I baptize you in the name of the Father, Son, and Holy Spirit." In more recent years, I have often adapted the baptismal formula of William Sloane Coffin: "I baptize you in the name of the Father, Son, and Holy Spirit, One God, Mother of us All."[1]

Then, as I bring them out of the water, I wait for them to wipe the water from their eyes and, looking at them face to face, I offer this prayer of blessing and commissioning:

May the Lord bless you and keep you.
May the Lord make his face to shine upon you
and be gracious to you.
May the Lord lift up his countenance upon you
And, *through you*, give the world peace. Amen.

A Benediction to the Reader

We come to the end of our journey into the meanings of baptism. Now, my readers, may the peace of God that passes all understanding keep your hearts and minds in Christ Jesus (Phil 4:7).

Note

1. Of the names used at baptism, the early church often baptized in the name of Jesus. By the time Matthew's Gospel was written, the trinitarian formula was used: Father, Son, and Holy Spirit. Jaroslav Pelikan, premier historian of doctrine, says that the trinitarian formula used at baptism from early years became the basis of the Apostles' Creed and the Nicene Creed, both of which use this formula as the outline of the creed. Coffin's adaptation affirms the ancient tradition, adds the Jewish foundational belief in the Oneness of God, and offers the name of Mother for God to express the feminine nature of God.

Appendix: Baptism Hymns and Spiritual Songs

1. "Baptized in Water, Sealed by the Spirit"
Michael Saward, 1981
BUNESSAN
The Worshipping Church (Carol Stream, IL: Hope Publishing Co., 1990), #758.

2. "Baptized into Your Name Most Holy"
J. J. Rambach, 1723
MENTZER
Rejoice in the Lord (Grand Rapids: Eerdmans, 1985), #529.

3. "Come Holy Spirit, Dove Divine"
Adoniram Judson, 1829
MARYTON
The Baptist Hymnal (Nashville: Convention Press, 1991), #364.

4. "In Water We Grow"
Brian Wren, 1989
LAUDATE DOMINUM or STANLEY BEACH
The Chalice Hymnal (St. Louis: Chalice, 1993), #364.

5. "I've Just Come from the Fountain"
African American Spiritual
HIS NAME SO SWEET
The Faith We Sing (Nashville: Abingdon, 2000), #2250.

6. "Take Me to the Water"
African American Spiritual
TAKE ME TO THE WATER
The Chalice Hymnal, #367, and *The African American Heritage Hymnal* (Chicago: KIA Publications, Inc., 2001), #675.

7. "This Is the Spirit's Entry Now"
Thomas E. Herbranson, 1965
PERRY
A New Hymnal for Colleges and Schools (New Haven: Yale University Press, 1992), #388.

8. "Wash, O God, Our Sons and Daughters"
Ruth Duck, 1987
BEACH SPRING
The United Methodist Hymnal (Nashville: United Methodist Publishing House, 1989), #605.

9. "Water, River, Spirit, Grace"
Thomas H. Troeger, 1987
TRES RIOS
The Faith We Sing, #2253

10. "We Know that Christ We Raised"
John B. Geyer, 1969
ENGELBURG
The United Methodist Hymnal, #610

11. "We Were Baptized in Christ Jesus"
John Ylvisaker, b. 1937
OUIMETE
The Faith We Sing, #2251.

12. "Will You Come and Follow Me"
John Bell and Graham Maule
Scottish Folk Melody, arranged by John Bell
The Church Hymnary (Norwich: Canterbury Press, 2005),
#533.